How to care for your
Palms and Ferns

Series editor: David Longman

Colour illustrations by Jane Fern

How to care for your
Palms and Ferns

by Tom Gough

Peter Lowe

THE AUTHOR

Tom Gough trained in horticulture with the famous houseplant
growers, Thomas Rochford and studied floristry both in Britain
and the Netherlands. He is chairman of Interflora, Greater
London and a director of a London florist company.

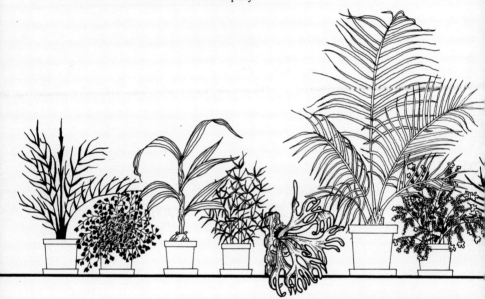

ISBN 0 85654 638 0

Printed in Italy by New Interlitho SpA

Contents

Common names

Scientific names

Introduction
How to use this book

This book describes the palms and ferns that you are likely to be able to obtain from the many retail outlets now selling houseplants, from specialist nurseries to motorway service stations. Each plant has a self-contained two-page entry. On the left is a general description of the plant with details of how to look after it, giving the correct amounts of water, light, warmth and humidity it needs, explaining how to clean and repot it and when and if it needs pruning. There is also a colour photo of a healthy leaf or frond. On the right hand page is a colour illustration of the plant showing all the things that can go wrong with it. Since this picture shows all the troubles at once, some of the plants look very sick indeed! To find out what is wrong with your plant, look for its symptoms on the illustration. Read the caption next to the part of the picture which shows the same features as your plant. It tells you what is wrong and how to put it right.

Palms are probably the most expensive houseplants that you are likely to acquire. Before buying one, read the care instructions to make sure you can provide the correct general conditions. Ferns, by comparison, can be among the least expensive of plants, although some of the varieties here are in the medium price range.

By no means do all plants require the same treatment, even if they come from the same general type. The Button fern *Pellaea rotundifolia,* for example, will soon die if the foliage is sprayed with water, yet the Sword fern *Nephrolepis exaltata* likes to be sprayed daily. *Chamaerops humilis,* the European fan palm, will take full sunlight but the almost identical-looking *Livistona chinensis,* the Chinese fan palm, will not tolerate direct sun. So whether you are beginning with a familiar fern or progressing to an exotic palm, always make sure you read the detailed care instructions for your plant and you will be able to look after it with confidence.

Tools for indoor gardening
It is possible to look after plants with the minimum of equipmen: a watering can, sprayer and plastic sponge are the real essenti; However, for long-term houseplant care, you will need a much more comprehensive collection, which can be acquired gradua as the need arises.

Keep separate sprayers and watering cans for insecticides and fungicides and a stock of basic insecticides. Methylated spirits is useful for removing some pests. Mark all containers used for insecticides clearly and wash them out regularly.

Leafshine can only be used on a few palms and ferns. Most palms are cleaned with a damp sponge or soft cloth. For delicate ferns, remove dust with a feather duster or dry paintbrush and spray with a fine mist. A paintbrush and cotton wool are useful for removing pests.

A small garden trowel and fork are useful when repotting or adding topsoil. A large spoon is a good substitute. A plastic bucket is essential for mixing composts, wetting peat and for giving very dry plants a thorough soaking.

Keep a selection of loam-based and peat-based composts, some pure moss or sedge peat. Some plants require lime-free mixtures. Sharp sand can be obtained from garden centres. Fertilizer, hormone rooting powder and charcoal are all useful.

Scissors, secateurs and a sharp knife are useful for removing dead or damaged fronds.

Two watering cans to which a rose can be attached are useful, one pint (½ litre) size, the other holding about a gallon (4½l). Never use your normal watering can for insecticides or fungicides.

Keep a small stock of flower pots and saucers, both plastic and clay. Old clay flower pots can be broken up to make excellent drainage material. Outer pots, with no drainage holes, can be used to hide the standard pot.

Twine, string, raffia and plant rings are essential for climbing plants, with a selection of canes, sticks and moss poles.

Watering and spraying

More houseplants are killed by incorrect watering (mainly of the little and often variety) than by anything else. Most prefer to be given a good soaking, then left almost to dry out before they are watered again. Some must be kept always moist – but in these cases the pot must be well drained so that the roots do not become waterlogged. Others prefer to dry out more thoroughly between waterings. Some need more water at one time of year than another. Always test the compost before watering to see how dry it is below the surface. In cold weather do not use cold water straight from the tap or the shock may damage the plant. Use tepid water for both watering and spraying.

Spraying keeps a plant's leaves clean and also provides extra humidity in hot, dry rooms. Avoid tap water if possible as the lime it contains clogs the pores of the leaves. Rainwater collected in a tank or bucket, water from melted ice in the freezer or boiled water which has been allowed to cool are all more suitable. Do not spray in bright sunlight as the water acts like a magnifying glass and may cause burn or scorch marks. A few plants dislike water on their leaves so before spraying you should check the individual requirements under each plant entry. Most, however benefit from a fine mist spray.

Feeding

Most composts contain fertilizer but for healthy growth plants also need extra nourishment, usually in spring and summer. Houseplant food or fertilizer is available as a liquid, diluted before use, as a powder added to water, as granules scattered on the surface of the soil and as a pill or stick pushed into the soil and gradually absorbed. You can also obtain a foliar feed which is sprayed onto the leaves. For most houseplants a liquid food is most suitable. It is clean, has no smell, and is easy and economical to use. There are several brands available and it is a good idea to try several and to change from time to time. Normally you

Watering

1. Test compost for dryness with finger or knife blade before watering. If blade comes out clean or soil dry and crumbly, compost is drying out. If soil sticks, it is still moist. Check instructions for each plant: some like a dry interval, others must be always moist.

2. Add water to top of compost, filling pot to the brim. Excess water will drain into saucer. After 15 minutes, empty any water remaining in the saucer. Do not allow pot to stand in water.

3. If plant is very dried out and does not mind water on its leaves, plunge pot into bowl so that water covers pot rim. Spray leaves. Leave for 15 minutes, then take it out and allow it to drain.

4. If plant cannot tolerate water on its leaves, add water to fill the saucer and wait for 15 minutes for it to be absorbed. Empty excess so that plant does not stand in water.

5. Or plunge pot into bowl or bucket of water to just below the pot rim. Leave it for 15 minutes, then take it out and allow it to drain.

Cleaning the leaves

1. Flick very dusty plants with a feather duster before cleaning.

2. Wipe leaves of palms with a damp cloth or sponge to remove dirt and revive the natural dull shine. Use soft water if possible and wipe the underside of the leaf as well as the top.

3. Clean ferns by misting or spraying with soft water. Check plant instructions first to make sure it will tolerate water on its leaves. Lime in hard tap water marks the leaves and clogs the pores. Do not spray in sunlight.

4. Most palms and ferns are damaged by leafshine but if it is recommended in the instructions, choose one based on vegetable oil, not an aerosol type. Do not use it more than once a month.

Humidity

Many palms and ferns require a high level of humidity, especially in hot, dry weather or in centrally heated rooms. A group of plants will create its own more humid atmosphere but you can improve the humidity around them in several ways.

1. Spray regularly with soft water, holding spray about 6in (15cm) from plant. Do not spray in strong sunlight or the leaves may burn.

When temperatures are high, most plants need more humidity. If temperature falls, they may need to be kept drier or some will rot. A few houseplants prefer a drier atmosphere all the year round. Check the instructions for each plant.

Self-watering planters

Self-watering planters are good for plants that need constant humidity. They are also useful when it is not possible to water regularly as their reservoirs will last up to six weeks before they need refilling. The compost takes in water gradually from a wick. The water evaporates slowly from the moist compost, raising humidity under the leaves. Like the wick in a paraffin heater, the wick of a self-watering planter absorbs its liquid at the same rate as it is used up, so that the compost never gets too wet. A gauge shows when more water is needed.

2. Stand pot on saucer full of pebbles almost covered in water. Do not let bottom of pot touch water or plant will become waterlogged and roots will rot away.

3. The pot can be placed inside a larger container with the space between the two packed with damp peat.

can simply follow the instructions on the bottle, adding a few drops to the water in the can when watering. For some plants, however, the mixture must be weaker than the manufacturer recommends on the bottle. If it is used at too concentrated a strength, it will damage the roots. Never increase the recommended strength and be careful with tablets and fertilizer sticks. If they are too close to the roots, the concentrated fertilizer may cause root damage.

If in doubt, don't feed. It is always better to slightly underfeed than to overfeed – and never feed a sick plant.

Repotting

Plants need repotting either because the roots have totally filled the existing pot and can no longer develop or because the nutritional value of the compost has been used up. It's quite easy to tell if a plant needs repotting. Remove it from its pot (see right). If there is a mass of roots and no soil showing, it needs repotting – it is pot-bound. If any soil is visible, don't repot. Replace plant in its old pot and gently firm it back in position. Other signs are roots growing through the pot base and weak, slow growth. Newly purchased plants should not normally need repotting. Do not repot unhealthy plants: the shock may kill them. In fact if in doubt, don't repot.

Repotting is usually done in spring – March or April in the northern hemisphere, September or October in the southern. Most plants require good drainage so that water can run through the compost freely and air can get to its roots. Broken crocks from old clay flower pots or a layer of coarse gravel at the bottom of the pot will provide drainage. Never use a container without drainage holes in its base. Put a piece of paper or a layer of moss over the drainage crocks to stop the compost from blocking the holes and inspect the root ball for pests. Remove old stones, damaged roots and old soil and gently remove old, loose compost from the top to a depth of about ½in (1cm). Then place plant in new pot.

After repotting, leave the plant without water for 2–3 days. The roots will spread out into the new compost in search of water. If it is very hot, spray the leaves every day.

Choosing the right compost: The correct type of compost or soil is very important for indoor plants. Don't use ordinary soil, which is usually too heavy and stifles the roots of young plants. Compost types vary considerably as some houseplants need a very light peat-based compost and some a heavy loam. The correct combination for each plant is given in the individual entries.

The two most commonly used types of compost are loam-based or peat-based. Loam-based compost is made up of sterilized loam (soil) mixed with peat and grit or coarse, washed sand. It is usually sold with fertilizer added, following formulae developed by the John Innes Institute for Horticultural Research. The numbers 1, 2 and 3 indicate the different proportions of fertilizer added. In this book they are referred to as 'loam-based No. 1, 2 or 3'. They are especially good for larger plants as they give more stability.

Peat-based composts are more open in

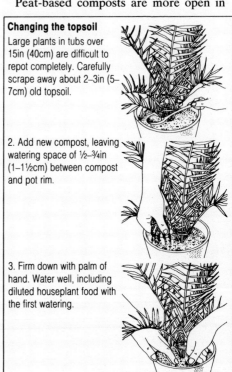

Changing the topsoil

Large plants in tubs over 15in (40cm) are difficult to repot completely. Carefully scrape away about 2–3in (5–7cm) old topsoil.

2. Add new compost, leaving watering space of ½–¾in (1–1½cm) between compost and pot rim.

3. Firm down with palm of hand. Water well, including diluted houseplant food with the first watering.

Repotting small plants

1. Find clean, dry pot, 1 size larger than old and add drainage layer, piece of paper or moss and little compost. Water plant well.

2. Hold pot upside down as shown and tap rim on edge of table to free root ball. If it sticks, tap in several places. Gently remove from pot. Scrape away loose soil and ½in (1cm) old topsoil.

3. Place root ball in new pot, fill with fresh compost, firming down with fingers or round stick. Do not press peat-based compost two hard.

4. Always leave ½–¾in (1–1½cm) watering space between compost and pot rim. Leave without water for 2–3 days. Do not feed for 2–3 weeks.

Bottle gardens

Bottle gardens provide a self-contained environment, and are ideal for most small ferns and palms as a very high level of humidity is produced. Like ships in bottles, they appear impossible to plant but with a simple home-made tool, can easily be set up. The bigger the bottle the better garden you will be able to make.

How to make a special tool

Using an old teaspoon and old kitchen fork, bend the bowl of the spoon so that it is at right angles to the handle, and bind the handles to the opposite ends of a strong cane, using insulating tape.

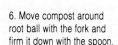

Planting a bottle garden

1. Make a sheet of paper into a cone shape. Place in neck of bottle. Pour in finely broken crocks or gravel, and a few grains of charcoal. Tip bottle to spread mixture evenly ½in (1cm) deep.

2. Add compost mixture to bottle, tipping so that the level is higher (5in, 13cm) one side than the other (3in, 9cm).

3. Use the fork end of your tool to move the compost about, then firm down with the back of the spoon.

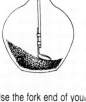

4. Decide where to place plants, taller plants at the back, shorter plants at the front. Dig a hole for each, starting at the back.

5. Knock plants from pots, and loosen compost from roots. Drop plants into holes.

6. Move compost around root ball with the fork and firm it down with the spoon.

7. Water so that water runs down the inside of the bottle wall to wash off excess compost. Wipe inside with a

cotton wool swab tied to the spoon. Do not use too much water, make soil just moist. Leave stopper off until condensation disappears. With stopper in place, enclosed environment will last without water for months.

Planting a self-watering planter

These are available in sizes from single pot size to large units for a mixture of plants. An 18in (45cm) square will take about five plants, including one up to 4ft (1.2m) high. A drainage layer is not necessary as the base of the soil compartment is perforated and there is a gap between this and the surface of the water below.

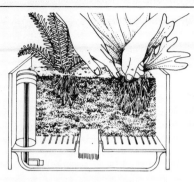

4. Fill planter with compost, leaving ¾in (1½cm) gap between top of soil and lip of planter. Firm down well around plants.

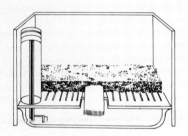

1. Place a layer of compost in the bottom of the planter.

2. Knock all plants out of their pots.

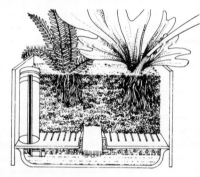

5. Pour water onto the soil. This will pass through the soil and soil compartment floor into the reservoir. Stop when the water gauge reads 'Maximum'.

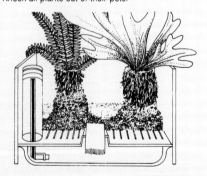

3. Place them in the planter so that the tops of their rootballs are level with each other, adjusting the level of the compost below each one.

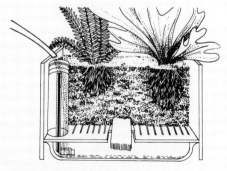

6. Water again by filling the reservoir when the indicator reads 0. Fill until it reads 'Maximum'.

texture, sterile, and hold moisture longer. They are normally composed of 10 parts of peat to 1 part of coarse sand with fertilizer added in the same proportions as loam-based compost. It is important when using peat composts not to firm them into the pot too hard. Plants absorb the fertilizer content more quickly from these composts than from loam-based ones. Sterilized peats, such as moss peat or sedge peat have no nutritional value but retain moisture.

Ericaceous or lime-free compost is available for plants that do not tolerate lime. Sphagnum moss is useful for some plants which are grown on cork bark or for lining a hanging basket. Sharp sand is fine, washed sand, available from garden centres. Do not use coarse builders' sand. It is sometimes mixed with loam to give a specially well-drained compost. Other useful items are small polystyrene balls to lighten the soil texture, rotted leafmould and manure.

Mixing compost: It mixing your own blend of compost, put the different items into a plastic bucket, using the same measure for each one. A plant pot or old cup will do. For 2 parts loam, 1 part peat, for example, fill the measure twice with loam, then once with peat. Mix the items together well with trowel or stick so that they are well blended.

Lighting

Palms and ferns need different amounts of light, but most prefer a high level of diffused daylight, but not direct sunlight. Diffused light is indirect sunlight, i.e. bouncing off a wall onto the plant or filtering through a net curtain.

Both in the northern and southern hemispheres, the sun rises in the east and sets in the west, but in the northern hemisphere in spring and autumn it shines at midday from the south, and in the southern hemisphere it shines at midday from the north. Plants placed in south-facing rooms in the northern hemisphere and in north-facing windows in the southern hemisphere, are therefore likely to receive the full rays of the sun at some time of day. Net curtains will help

to shield your plant from these rays, but better still, place them well away from the window, though not in a dark corner!

Conversely south-facing rooms in the southern hemisphere, and north-facing rooms in the northern hemisphere tend to be dull and only suitable for shade-loving plants as the sun will never shine through the window.

Artificial light: To compensate for lack of daylight you can install fluorescent tubes or spotlights. However, conventional artificial light is not as intense as natural daylight and certain plants will not thrive under artificial light.

This problem occurs particularly in offices where either the windows are covered with a solar screen, or where there are no windows at all.

Special horticultural spotlights and fluorescent tubes are available which imitate diffused sunlight more closely and these have a good effect on plants. Their main drawback is that the tubes produce a very stark light and spotlights produce heat which, if focussed onto the plants, will burn their delicate leaves. For the technically minded there are other types of lamp such as mercury vapour, metal halide and low pressure sodium but for the home and office, tubes and spotlights are the most practical.

Spotlights: To imitate diffused daylight, a blue coating is added to the front of the bulb. The light seems the same as that of a conventional spotlight but in practice plants do actually grow as though they are in daylight. Unfortunately, the problem of heat has not been solved. A 150w reflector lamp mounted closer than 39in (1m) to the plant will overheat its leaves. At 39in (1m) sufficient light will be produced over an area 39in (1m) in diameter but at a distance of 78in (2m), only a quarter of that light will fall on the leaves. Although it is sometimes difficult to position the lights so as to get enough light and not too much heat, spotlights are probably the most adaptable types to use.

Pruning and trimming

Palms cannot be pruned to prevent further growth since they produce only one new frond at a time and older fronds gradually die. If new growth is removed, the whole plant will eventually die.

1. Remove old, dead leaves by cutting off as close to the trunk or stem as possible with a sharp knife.

2. In time the stump of the leaf stem will fall off, creating an attractive herringbone pattern on the trunk.

Ferns may become bushy and older leaves can be removed with a pair of sharp scissors if absolutely necessary for space reasons.

Do not pinch out ferns or palms to try to make them bushy. It will stunt growth. If tips of leaves or fronds turn brown and dry, they can be removed with sharp scissors. Cut just inside brown area to avoid damaging healthy tissue.

Propagation

It is possible to propagate some ferns from their spores, using a heated propagator but for most, root division is the most successful way of increasing your stock.

1. A plant that has become very bushy can be divided into 2, 3 or even 4 parts. First prepare as many smaller pots as you need – see Repotting (p.10).

3. Gently pull roots and stems apart with your hands.

4. For a very pot-bound plant with a mass of roots, use a sharp knife.

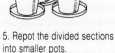

2. Remove plant from pot and shake away loose soil.

5. Repot the divided sections into smaller pots.

Fluorescent lights: These are a much more efficient method of providing light and are a popular source of office lighting. They do not give out much heat and are available with a wide range of intensities. Special horticultural tubes fit standard fittings and are available in the same lengths as conventional tubes. They can be used with standard tubes to give a less stark light. They are obviously not so flexible as spotlights as far as positioning goes, but if a combination of the two types is used, plants in darker areas will benefit. Most specialist plant shops will be able to advise you about what is available and give more detailed technical information.

Insecticides

Unfortunately some houseplants are vulnerable to pests and diseases. The most common are mealy bug, scale insect, red spider mite and green or whitefly. These should be treated as soon as they are noticed and affected plants moved away from others to prevent the spread of infection. Plants with thin, delicate leaves, are attacked by insects such as red spider mite while greenfly are attracted to young leaves and stems. Some pests, such as mealy bug, appear on the leaves but may be carried hidden in the soil.

Insecticides are available usually as concentrated liquids which are added to water and sprayed or watered onto the infected plant, and as aerosols ready for use. Less usually, some chemicals for houseplants come in powdered form. This is not suitable for all plants – check the individual instructions. Systemic insecticides are absorbed into the plant's veins (its system) and so spread the poison to any insect which tries to take nourishment from these.

The least toxic insecticides are those based on pyrethrum and derris as these are both natural substances. They are most suited to whitefly and greenfly control. Derris is also suitable for whitefly and greenfly and controls red spider mite in the early stages. Methylated spirits can be used to remove scale insect and mealy bugs. Red spider can be prevented from recurring by improving humidity. Malathion is one of the most effective general insecticides and will control everything from whitefly to beetles, and especially mealy bug which is one of the most infectious and damaging insects likely to affect houseplants. Other insects such as scale insect and thrips can also be controlled by spraying malathion. It can be sprayed when diluted and also watered into the soil if the soil is infected.

Malathion may damage some sensitive plants, so read the captions carefully to make sure you choose the right treatment for your plant.

Generally insecticides should be applied every 14 days until the pest disappears – but see the instructions for each plant. Fungicides, for mould and fungus infections, generally work with only one application. Check new plants for pests, as they quickly spread from plant to plant. A preventative spray in spring will guard against attack.

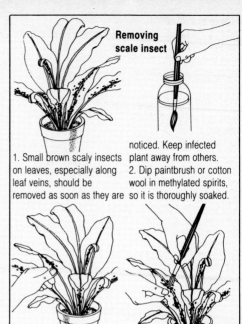

Removing scale insect

1. Small brown scaly insects on leaves, especially along leaf veins, should be removed as soon as they are noticed. Keep infected plant away from others.
2. Dip paintbrush or cotton wool in methylated spirits, so it is thoroughly soaked.

3. Dab each scale insect with methylated spirits to loosen it.
4. Remove with thumbnail. Make sure all insects are removed.

Taking care with insecticides

Insecticides and fungicides may contain deadly chemicals. Use them with care.
Never mix different types of insecticides as the chemicals may react.
Never put them into other bottles, such as soft drink or beer bottles.
Never breathe in the spray.
Never spray in windy weather.
Never pour them down the sink or drains. Do not even pour the water in which you have washed containers and sprayers down the drain.
Never make up more at one time than you will use.
Never keep diluted insecticide for more than 24 hours.
Never leave old containers lying around.
Always follow instructions carefully. Do not over or under dilute.

Always use a separate watering can and sprayer, keeping another one for normal spraying and watering.
Always keep away from food, crockery, glasses, food containers, and minerals. Derris is harmful to fish; malathion harms bees.
Always cover fish bowls when spraying.
Always store them with their sprayers and containers in a dry, frost free place, on a high shelf out of reach of children.
Always spray outside, in the evening when bees are not around.
Always wash out all sprayers and empty bottles after use, inside and out.
Always pour washing water onto ground away from food crops and water sources such as streams and rivers.
Always throw empty bottles and containers away with domestic waste.
Always wash thoroughly in hot water and detergent when you have used them.

Parlour palm

Sometimes known as *Neanthe bella*, this plant must not be confused with rather similar *Kentia* varieties. It is an easy plant to grow in the house, reaching a maximum height of only 3ft–3ft 6in (90–115cm) with fronds 9–24in (22–60cm) long. It can become quite bushy with age. At 3 or more years old it can produce a flower spike, not unlike mimosa. The florets will develop into small berry-like fruits. The parlour palm is particularly susceptible to red spider. Scale insect and mealy bug are less common, but they must be looked out for.

The Parlour palm's soft dark green leaves grow from a stem between 9–24in (22–60cm) long. Their slightly glossy appearance can be maintained using liquid leafshines, but not aerosol types. A daily spray with soft water will keep them clean and provide the high humidity they need.

Light: High level of diffused light (see p. 13), but not full sun, which dries out leaves. Will survive a long time in a relatively dark place.

Temperature: Winter minimum 55°F (13°C), summer minimum 60°F (16°C), summer maximum 65°F (18°C).

Water: Keep moist at all times, watering 2–3 times a week in summer, once a week in winter.

Humidity: Spray daily with rainwater or soft water. Stand pot in saucer on pebbles almost covered with water. Steamy kitchen or bathroom are good situations.

Feeding: Every 14 days in summer only, with houseplant food diluted with water. Use half the amount recommended by the maker. (See p. 8.)

Soil: Mixture of 2 parts loam-based No. 1 and 1 part peat.

Repotting: Every year in spring, into pot one size larger. If more than 1 plant growing together, do not separate roots.

Cleaning: Once every 2 months with vegetable-based oil cleaner diluted according to maker's instructions, with milk (use 6–7 drops in a cup of water) or with liquid leafshine. No aerosol leafshine. Between cleanings, wipe with damp cloth.

Removing dead fronds

If whole fronds are dry and discoloured, cut them off with sharp knife or secateurs close to the main stem.

Removing the flower spike

After producing berries, the spike will wither and dry. Cut it off with scissors as close to the stem as possible. If you have a heated propagator you can try to grow new plants from the seeds. They need a temperature of 80°F (27°C) to germinate.

what goes wrong

Small flat discs sticking to underside of leaves. Scale insect. Paint with methylated spirits and remove with thumbnail or spray every 14 days with diluted malathion.

Leaves turn yellow and have webs underneath. Red spider mite. Spray with diluted malathion or a systemic insecticide every 14 days until clear.

White woolly patches on leaves and stems. Mealy bug. Paint with methylated spirits and remove with thumbnail or spray with derris, diluted malathion or systemic insecticide every 14 days until clear.

Plant does not grow. Too cold and wet or needs feeding. Check and correct conditions. Move to warmer place and allow to dry out before watering again. Feed every 14 days in summer with food at half recommended strength.

Whole fronds turn brown, dry up and die. Air too dry. Stand pot on wet pebbles or put in outer pot packed with damp peat. Also caused by overfeeding. Feed every 14 days in summer only, with food at half recommended strength.

Tips of leaves turn brown. Too hot or in too sunny a position. Move to a position in indirect sunlight; water and remember to spray regularly with soft water. Can also be leafshine damage. Do not use.

Leaves rot at soil level and fall. Too cold and wet. Move to warmer room and allow to dry out before watering again.

European fan palm

This is Europe's only native palm and, although plants may vary in leaf size and shape, they all belong to a single species. It makes an ideal houseplant, especially in unheated rooms. It can reach 20ft (6m) in height but indoors is usually only 4ft (120cm) tall with leaves up to 2ft (60cm) across. It starts life with its fan-shaped leaves growing straight from the soil. As it produces new leaves, old ones die and fall off, the process producing a trunk which has stiff dark fibres near the crown. Young leaves are covered with pale woolly down which disappears as they grow.

When young, the European fan palm's dark green fan-shaped leaves grow on stems straight from the compost. As they grow older, a trunk forms with leaf stems radiating from its top. They need full sunlight and weekly feeding in summer to grow well.

Light: Full sunlight. Shade badly affects growth of new leaves.

Temperature: Autumn–spring, 40–50°F (4–10°C); spring–autumn, 50–60°F (10–16°C).

Water: 3 times a week in summer to keep moist, twice a week in winter. If large plant, in pot 7in (17cm) or more, may need daily watering in summer.

Humidity: Spray with soft water every week in centrally heated rooms. Planting in self-watering planter or with other plants keeps humidity adequate.

Feeding: Weekly in summer with house-plant food diluted with water according to maker's instructions. (See p. 8.)

Soil: 2 parts loam-based No. 2, 1 part decayed leafmould and sand. Good drainage essential.

Repotting: Annually in spring for young plants. When 4ft (120cm) tall, pot up into 20in (50cm) container then change top soil annually.

Cleaning: Spray with soft water. Wipe older (not young down-covered) leaves with damp sponge. No aerosol leafshine.

Webs under leaves. Red spider mite. Spray leaves with half-strength malathion-based insecticide every 14 days until clear. Increase humidity.

Watering

1. The plant should be kept always moist in summer. Test compost with your finger. If dry and crumbly, plant needs watering. If very dry, surface may be hard.

2. Fill space between compost and top of pot with water and allow to drain through. Leave for 15 minutes, then throw excess water away.

New fronds do not open. Too dark or too dry in summer. If in shade, move to sun-facing room or place near light window. In summer keep moist by watering at least 3 times a week – but do not stand in water.

New leaf tips turn brown. Needs water. Keep plant moist all the time in summer. Slight browning at tip is natural.

All leaves dry out. Too hot. Keep room well ventilated and do not exceed 60°F (16°C) in summer, 50°F (10°C) in winter.

what goes wrong

No new fronds appear. Needs feeding or soil replacing. If adult, change top soil. If young, repot in spring. Feed every week in summer.

New fronds grow slowly and are yellowish. Plant waterlogged. Check pot is not standing in water and has sufficient drainage in bottom.

Leaves turn black. Too cold. If outside, frosted. Move indoors if outside and if in cool greenhouse, provide heater if under 40°F (4°C). Black patches caused by spraying fronds with too concentrated malathion.

Leaves have brown patches. Leafshine damage. Do not use aerosol type. Clean leaves with damp sponge

Oldest leaves dry out. Air too dry. Down on younger leaves helps to retain moisture. Put plant in outer container packed with damp peat, especially if in centrally heated room. Spray weekly.

Brown discs on leaves and stems. Scale insect. Paint with methylated spirits and remove with thumbnail.

White woolly patches where frond joins trunk. Mealy bug. Every 14 days add liquid malathion to water. Spray stem with half-strength malathion every 14 days until clear.

19

Chrysalidocarpus lutescens

Areca palm

This extremely graceful palm, some-times known as *Areca lutescens*, has rich, soft green leaves deeply divided into long narrow segments. The plants grow in dense clusters and throw off extra trunks as suckers, which can be allowed to grow with the original pro-vided the plants are not overcrowded. Usually, these suckers completely ob-scure the trunk. Up to 25ft (7½m) tall in its natural habitat, the Areca palm is sold as a houseplant between 2 and 3ft (60–90cm).

Light: Plenty needed, but should be pro-tected from strong sun. Will tolerate shade.

Temperature: Winter minimum 50°F (10°C), though happier with 60°F (16°C). Summer maximum 80°F (27°C), though ideal is 70°F (21°C).

Water: 3 times a week in summer. In winter, once every week to 10 days, allow-ing soil almost to dry out between water-ings.

Humidity: Spray with fine mist twice a week in summer, once in winter. When over 75°F (24°C), spray daily. Stand on a saucer of pebbles almost covered with water.

Feeding: Weekly in spring and summer with houseplant food diluted with water according to maker's instructions. (See p. 8.)

Soil: For young plant, a mixture of 1 part loam-based No. 1 and 1 part peat. For plants over 3 years old, equal parts of loam and sand, with added rotted horse or cow manure (about ⅕ of total mixture).

Repotting: Annually in spring, into plastic pot one size larger, disturbing roots as little as possible. Use broken crocks for good drainage in pot.

Cleaning: Carefully wipe with sponge or damp cloth. No leafshine.

A healthy Areca palm has rich, soft green fronds and yellow stems. Suckers grow straight from the compost and hide the stems with their fronds. Unless the pot becomes overcrowded, these can be retained to give an attractive display.

All leaves on frond go brown. Root damage caused by knocking over plant or repotting at wrong time of year. Cut off dead stem at soil surface. New suckers will soon grow.

what goes wrong

Individual leaves turn brown. Leafshine damage. Do not use any kind. Clean only with water.

20

White woolly patches on leaf joints. Mealy bug. Add malathion to water every 14 days until clear. Paint woolly patches with methylated spirits. Do not use malathion on leaves.

Leaves turn pale. Waterlogged. Do not allow to stand in water. In winter allow soil almost to dry out between waterings.

Round spots on leaves, discs underneath. Scale insect. Paint with methylated spirits and remove with thumbnail.

Leaves dry out from tips. Too hot. Move to cooler place and spray regularly.

New leaves do not develop properly. Needs feeding. Feed every week in spring and summer, the growing season.

Webs and small insects under leaves. Red spider mite. Spray under leaves with pyrethum-based insecticide and add malathion to water every 14 days until clear.

Leaves dry out from tips. Too hot and air too dry. Move to cooler place and spray daily if over 70°F (21°C).

Stems turn yellow. This is natural, as plant matures.

All leaves droop. Needs water. Water well and spray at once. Keep always moist in summer; in winter do not allow to dry out completely.

All leaves turn black. Too cold. Move to warmer place. Winter minimum 50°F (10°C), summer minimum 60°F (16°C).

21

Cocos nucifera

Coconut palm

This palm has rather sparse foliage which grows out of a half-visible coconut. The leaves are long and grouped two to a frond, appearing to grow straight from the nut. As the plant develops, lower fronds die and new ones grow from the top of the central stem, in time producing a trunk. It is a slow grower, usually bought for its novelty. Its main problem is a rotting nut, usually caused by too frequent or over watering.

Light: Full sunlight. Care needed when spraying as water drips left on leaves can act as magnifying glasses, burning them.

Temperature: Winter minimum 65°F (18°C). Tolerates up to 80°F (27°C) in summer.

Water: Keep just moist, watering once or twice a week in summer, once a week in winter. Do not get water on nut or stand pot in water.

Humidity: Should be high. Stand pot in saucer of pebbles almost covered with water, or put pot into larger one with damp peat between the two.

Feeding: Every 3 weeks in summer with houseplant food diluted with water. Use half the amount recommended by the maker. (See p. 8.)

Soil: Mixture of 2 parts loam-based No. 2, 1 part peat, 1 part sand. Include small amount of vermiculite balls if available, e.g. 1 eggcup full in 7in (17cm) pot. Good drainage essential.

Repotting: Only when entirely pot-bound, into pot one size larger. Otherwise, leave roots undisturbed and replace 1in (2½cm) of topsoil with soil mixture above. A heavier loam required for a very large plant (6ft, 2m), 3 parts loam-based No. 2 to 1 part peat and 1 part sand.

Cleaning: Wipe with damp cloth. No leafshine.

The Coconut palm produces dramatic, though sparse, green foliage with leaves grouped two to a frond. The nut from which the fronds grow lies half buried in the compost and should never be allowed to get wet. When spraying the fronds, be careful not to get moisture on the nut.

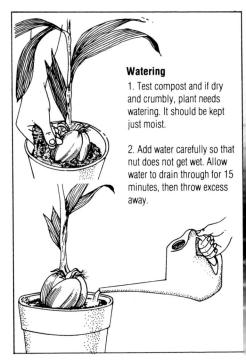

Watering

1. Test compost and if dry and crumbly, plant needs watering. It should be kept just moist.

2. Add water carefully so that nut does not get wet. Allow water to drain through for 15 minutes, then throw excess away.

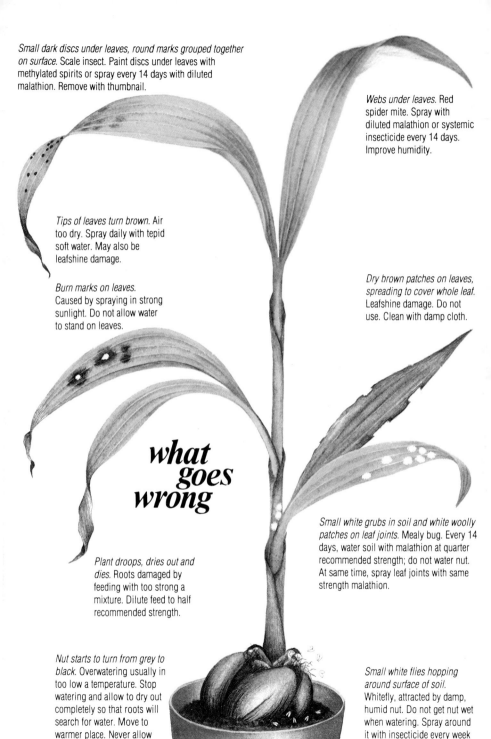

Small dark discs under leaves, round marks grouped together on surface. Scale insect. Paint discs under leaves with methylated spirits or spray every 14 days with diluted malathion. Remove with thumbnail.

Webs under leaves. Red spider mite. Spray with diluted malathion or systemic insecticide every 14 days. Improve humidity.

Tips of leaves turn brown. Air too dry. Spray daily with tepid soft water. May also be leafshine damage.

Burn marks on leaves. Caused by spraying in strong sunlight. Do not allow water to stand on leaves.

Dry brown patches on leaves, spreading to cover whole leaf. Leafshine damage. Do not use. Clean with damp cloth.

what goes wrong

Plant droops, dries out and dies. Roots damaged by feeding with too strong a mixture. Dilute feed to half recommended strength.

Small white grubs in soil and white woolly patches on leaf joints. Mealy bug. Every 14 days, water soil with malathion at quarter recommended strength; do not water nut. At same time, spray leaf joints with same strength malathion.

Nut starts to turn from grey to black. Overwatering usually in too low a temperature. Stop watering and allow to dry out completely so that roots will search for water. Move to warmer place. Never allow water to get on nut.

Small white flies hopping around surface of soil. Whitefly, attracted by damp, humid nut. Do not get nut wet when watering. Spray around it with insecticide every week until clear.

23

Cocos weddeliana

Dwarf coconut palm

This is an attractive, deceptively delicate-looking house palm, grown for its foliage as it will not produce coconut fruits. In fact, it is tough and relatively easy to care for. Requiring a humid atmosphere, it is usually grown several to a pot and, since it grows slowly, is an ideal bottle garden plant. It dislikes having its roots disturbed. It is sometimes known as *Microcoelum* or *Syagrus weddeliana.*

Light: Tolerates high level of light, including direct sunlight. If daylight insufficient, use an artificial light to improve growth. (See p. 13.)

Temperature: Winter minimum 60°F (16°C), summer maximum 70°F (21°C).

Water: In summer keep moist, but not saturated, watering 2 or 3 times a week. In winter allow almost to dry out between waterings, every week to 10 days.

Humidity: Spray twice a week with fine mist of tepid soft water. Stand in saucer of pebbles almost covered with water. The humid microclimate of a bottle-garden (See p. 11) is ideal.

Feeding: Once every 2 to 3 weeks in summer with houseplant food diluted with water. Use half the amount recommended by the maker. (See p. 8.)

Soil: Mixture of 3 parts loam-based No. 1 and 1 part sedge or moss peat.

Repotting: Annually in early spring into clay pot one size larger. Knock root-ball out whole. If several are planted together, do not separate root-balls.

Cleaning: Wipe both sides of leaves every week with damp cloth and tepid, soft water. No leafshine.

Removing fronds: Cut off brown and shrivelled lower leaves with scissors or secateurs as close as possible to main stem.

The Dwarf coconut palm has delicate-looking green fronds. It grows slowly, and several plants are usually placed together in one pot to give a more bushy appearance. It is a relatively easy plant, but does require a humid atmosphere.

Leaf tips turn brown. Air too dry. Spray daily with tepid soft water in a fine mist. Avoid large droplets which may mark leaves.

New leaves dry up. Too hot. Do not exceed 70°F (21°C) unless there is good circulation of air. Spray weekly with tepid soft water to improve humidity. If plant also not growing in summer, check not standing in water. Allow to dry out before watering again.

Whole plant dries up. Roots disturbed. Has it been knocked over? Carefully firm soil back into pot and continue watering as usual. Repot carefully following spring if plant survives.

Plant does not grow. Too dark. Needs bright light all year round. If already in good position, may need repotting. Repot in following spring and feed regularly meanwhile.

what goes wrong

New leaves turn brown. Too cold. Move to warmer place, at least 60°F (16°C).

Repotting

Repot in spring when roots growing through pot and lack of new fronds show soil nutrients are used up. Prepare pot 1 size larger with drainage material and compost. Palms prefer tall, narrow pots.

1. Remove plant from pot.

2. Carefully remove stale soil from roots, using stick or pencil.

3. Place plant in centre of new pot, root-ball on compost.

4. Add new compost to fill pot. Make sure that all roots are covered. Leave in the shade without water for 2 days to encourage roots to grow into compost.

Some leaves have brown patches. Leafshine damage. Do not use. Clean both sides of leaves with tepid water only.

Lower leaves dry and crisp. Needs water. Plunge pot into bucket of water until bubbles stop rising. Drain thoroughly before replacing in position.

Sago palm

This palm-like plant has a woody trunk and a head of stiff, spiny, gracefully arching fronds. Ideal for cool or warm greenhouses, it grows happily in the house. When 10 to 15 years old, it can be 6ft (nearly 2m) in diameter with leaves 2–3ft (60–90cm) long. Young plants are usually 2ft (60cm) high and do not yet have a trunk, the fronds radiating from the surface of the soil. In spring, the plant forms a circle of new fronds. Old fronds may then turn yellowy brown and fall off.

One of the oldest forms of vegetation known to man, these plants formed the staple diet of the dinosaurs.

Light: Shaded, in diffused daylight (see p. 13), in summer. Full light in winter. Do not move plant round, or the change in light angle will make leaves misshapen.

Temperature: Winter minimum 60°F (16°C), summer average 70°F (21°C). Increase to 75°F (24°C) when circle of new fronds is forming.

Water: Daily in summer, twice weekly in winter. Good drainage essential.

Humidity: Spray daily with tepid soft water in summer, twice weekly in winter. Stand young plant on saucer of pebbles almost covered with water. Mature plant benefits from being in self-watering container.

Feeding: Weekly in summer with houseplant food diluted with water according to maker's instructions. (See p. 8.)

Soil: Equal parts of loam-based No. 2 and sharp sand. Put broken crocks in bottom of pot.

Repotting: Annually in spring for young plants. When too large to repot, replace topsoil.

Cleaning: Wipe with damp cloth weekly. Use liquid leafshine once every 2 months. No aerosol leafshine.

The spiny, arched fronds of the Sago palm radiate from a central core which will in time develop into a woody trunk. A healthy plant has dark green fronds but new leaves are pale, maturing if kept in good indirect light. Strong sun turns the leaves pale brown.

Cutting off dead fronds
Cut off brown, dead fronds as close to trunk as possible with secateurs. The stumps will form the trunk.

Leaves dry out, turn yellowish brown and drop. Natural on older fronds when new ones forming. Cut off brown fronds with secateurs as near to trunk as possible. If new leaves turn colour, air too dry or too hot. Spray daily and move to cooler place.

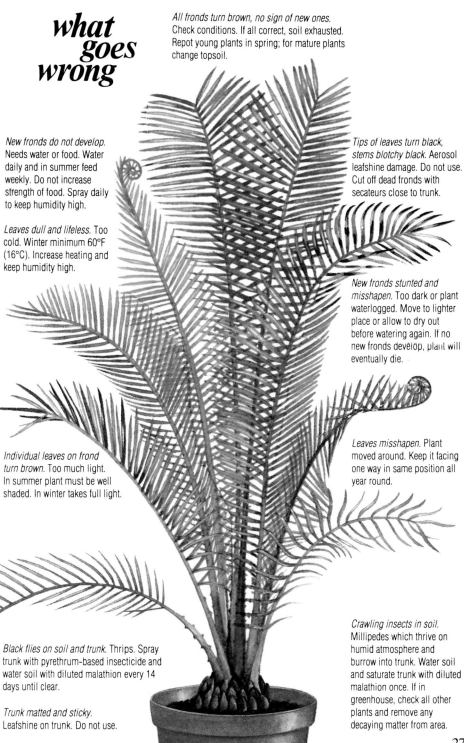

what goes wrong

All fronds turn brown, no sign of new ones. Check conditions. If all correct, soil exhausted. Repot young plants in spring; for mature plants change topsoil.

New fronds do not develop. Needs water or food. Water daily and in summer feed weekly. Do not increase strength of food. Spray daily to keep humidity high.

Leaves dull and lifeless. Too cold. Winter minimum 60°F (16°C). Increase heating and keep humidity high.

Individual leaves on frond turn brown. Too much light. In summer plant must be well shaded. In winter takes full light.

Black flies on soil and trunk. Thrips. Spray trunk with pyrethrum-based insecticide and water soil with diluted malathion every 14 days until clear.

Trunk matted and sticky. Leafshine on trunk. Do not use.

Tips of leaves turn black, stems blotchy black. Aerosol leafshine damage. Do not use. Cut off dead fronds with secateurs close to trunk.

New fronds stunted and misshapen. Too dark or plant waterlogged. Move to lighter place or allow to dry out before watering again. If no new fronds develop, plant will eventually die.

Leaves misshapen. Plant moved around. Keep it facing one way in same position all year round.

Crawling insects in soil. Millipedes which thrive on humid atmosphere and burrow into trunk. Water soil and saturate trunk with diluted malathion once. If in greenhouse, check all other plants and remove any decaying matter from area.

Kentia forsteriana

Paradise palm

Sometimes called *Howea forsteriana*, after the Lord Howe Islands, this is the 'Victorian' palm associated with palm courts. Mature specimens can grow to 12ft (over 3m) in the home. As *K. forsteriana* is very slow-growing, producing one leaf per plant per year, it is usually planted three or four to a pot. It is extremely tolerant of various light conditions and will survive in a dark situation for a long time. It is very susceptible to root damage if knocked over, so treat it with care.

Light: Indirect daylight preferred, but survives quite well in artificial light (see p. 13).
Temperature: Winter minimum 50°F (10°C), summer maximum 75°F (24°C).
Water: In summer, keep just moist at all times, watering once or twice a week. In winter, once every week or ten days, allowing almost to dry out in between.
Humidity: Spray daily with fine mist of tepid soft water in summer, especially if 75°F (24°C) or over.
Feeding: Every 14 days in summer with houseplant food diluted with water according to maker's instructions. (See p. 8.)
Soil: Fibrous mixture of 4 parts loam-based No. 2, 1 part sedge or moss peat, 1 part rotted pine needles.
Repotting: In spring, only if plant is pot-bound, into pot one size larger. With younger plant, knock from its pot very carefully, ensuring root-ball does not crumble or the individual plants separate. With large, mature plants, do not repot, just change topsoil.
Cleaning: Wipe every week with damp cloth. Use vegetable-based oil cleaner, 6–7 drops of milk in a cup of soft water, or liquid leafshine diluted in water (make it 4 times weaker than the maker's recommended strength). No aerosol leafshine.

The Paradise palm's long, graceful fronds develop from a leaf spike which unfurls slowly. It grows at the rate of only one new frond a year. It needs good, indirect light but will grow well in artificial light, too. As with other slow-growing palms, several plants are often placed together in one pot.

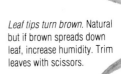

Leaf tips turn brown. Natural but if brown spreads down leaf, increase humidity. Trim leaves with scissors.

Trimming the fronds and leaves
Cut out dead lower fronds. Cut as close to main stem as possible.
If the tips of the leaves are brown and dry, trim them off with sharp scissors, cutting just outside healthy leaf tissue.

what goes wrong

New frond does not unfurl.
Too dark and air too dry.
Move to lighter place (not
direct sun) and keep moist in
summer. Spray daily with
tepid soft water.

Silver and black marks on
leaves. Thrips. Spray every 14
days with diluted malathion
until clear.

Brown patches on leaves.
Leafshine damage. Do not
use aerosol type. Use only
water or vegetable-oil based
cleaner.

New leaf spike turns black.
Too cold – new leaves are
damaged first. Move to
warmer place (at least 50°F,
10°C). In winter allow soil
almost to dry out between
waterings.

New leaf smaller than adult
leaves. Needs feeding. Feed
every 14 days in summer.

One plant dries up leaving
others healthy. Root damage
– plant may have been knocked,
and too high a temperature.
Remove dead plant.

Brown discs on underside of leaves. Scale
insect. Paint with methylated spirits and
remove with thumbnail or spray with diluted
malathion every 14 days until clear.

Older leaves dry up. Too hot.
Do not exceed 75°F (24°C).
Move to cooler place and
water and spray regularly.

Plant goes black and rots at
base. Too wet, overwatered.
May die but allow to dry out
completely and move to
warm, light position.

Whole plant dries out. Needs
water, especially in summer
when plant should be moist at
all times.

Chinese fan palm

This house palm, popular in many countries, is very decorative when young, with fan-like leaves divided half-way to the centre into long pointed segments growing on a stiff stem which rises from the centre of the plant. A mature plant can grow as high as 30ft (8m) with leaves 6ft (over 1½m) across. In their natural habitat, the leaves of some varieties are used for roofing and hats, and the leaf bases for rope. Although almost hardy, it will not tolerate frost. As a houseplant it is usually about 3ft (90cm) tall when bought. It grows very slowly to about 6ft (1½m), its trunk forming from the dead leaf sheaths.

Light: Full light, though keep out of summer sun. Shade slows growth.

Temperature: Winter minimum 50°F (10°C), summer minimum 60°F (15°C). Best all-round temperature is 65–70°F (18–22°C), with 75°F (24°C) summer maximum.

Water: Every day in summer, including trunk, to keep soil moist at all times. In winter once or twice a week.

Humidity: Spray once a week. Stand young plant on saucer of pebbles almost covered with water to increase humidity.

Feeding: Weekly in spring and summer with houseplant food diluted with water according to maker's instructions. (See p. 8.)

Soil: Equal parts loam-based No. 3, decayed stable manure. Good drainage essential.

Repotting: Annually in spring into well-drained pots for young plants. Change topsoil for larger, adult plants. Feed after changing topsoil but after complete repotting, do not feed for 2 weeks.

Cleaning: Wipe with damp cloth or sponge. No leafshine.

The Chinese fan palm has leathery, slightly glossy leaves which grow like large green fans. The pointed segments are joined together from the leaf base to about half way up and have wispy threads hanging between the points.

Brown discs on leaves and stems. Scale insect. Paint with methylated spirits and remove with thumbnail. Stems but not leaves can be sprayed with malathion every 14 days until clear.

what goes wrong

White woolly patches where frond joins trunk. Mealy bug. Water soil with liquid malathion diluted as recommended. Spray stems with same solution but do not spray leaves or they will 'burn'.

Webs under leaves. Red spider mite. Wipe with cloth dipped in pyrethrum-based insecticide diluted to half normal strength every week until clear. Do not use nicotine or malathion or leaves will burn.

No new fronds grow. Soil nutrients used up. If young plant, repot in spring. If adult, change topsoil. Feed regularly.

Leaves grow slowly and turn yellow. Too wet, badly drained. Allow to dry out before watering again and check drainage in pot.

New fronds do not open. Too dark or needs water. Move to lighter room or place near light window. Keep moist in summer, watering every day if soil dries quickly. Do not stand in water.

New leaf tips turn brown. Some browning natural but if all tips brown, needs watering. Keep moist in summer.

Brown patches on leaves. Leafshine damage. Do not use.

Leaves turn black. Too cold. If outside for summer, bring in if temperature falls below 50°F (10°C).

Leaves dry out. Too hot. Do not exceed 75°F (24°C) and in summer keep room well ventilated. 65–70°F (18–21°C) best. Oldest fronds will dry out eventually and if rest are healthy this is natural. Remove dead ones by cutting off with secateurs as close to trunk as possible.

31

Canary Island date palm

This plant requires a large home since it grows to 15ft (4½m) as a house-plant. It is a very chunky plant when mature with a large and heavy root ball: an 8-ft (2½m) specimen could weigh as much as 3cwt (152kg) and would need to be planted in a pot the size of a small dustbin! As it develops, a trunk forms as the lower leaves die. These should be removed with a saw or very sharp knife. The palm will stand quite low temperatures, and can be put outside in the summer even in northern countries. They grow slowly ; about 6–10in (15–25cm) a year.

The Canary Island date palm has pale green new leaves which turn darker green as they mature and develop and may have brown, fibrous hair at the edges. Healthy leaves have a natural gloss but should never be treated with leafshine or they will turn black and dry out.

Light: Indirect daylight when young; takes full sunlight when over 4 years old.
Temperature: Cool in winter – about 50°F (10°C). Summer maximum 80°F (27°C), allowing plenty of fresh air round plant if very hot.
Water: At least twice a week in summer to keep evenly moist. In winter water only when surface soil appears dry, about once in 14 days.
Humidity: Spray twice a week with tepid water if temperature over 80°F (27°C). Do not spray in winter.
Feeding: Every 14 days in summer with liquid houseplant food diluted with water according to maker's instructions. (See p. 8.)
Soil: Heavy, peatless loam like loam-based No. 3. Use reddish clay/loam for larger plants from southern Europe.
Repotting: Annually for small specimens. With larger specimens in planters, change topsoil.
Cleaning: Spray with tepid soft water, or use household duster on a stick to keep your distance from sharp leaves. No leaf-shine.

Changing the topsoil

1. In spring soil will need renewing. Remove top 2in (5cm) with trowel, being careful not to damage roots.

2. Replace with new compost. Firm gently around roots. Do not water for 2 days, to encourage roots to grow into new soil. Feed regularly.

Bottom fronds dry up. Natural as long as rest stay healthy. Remove old dead frond with sharp knife or saw, cutting as close to trunk as possible.

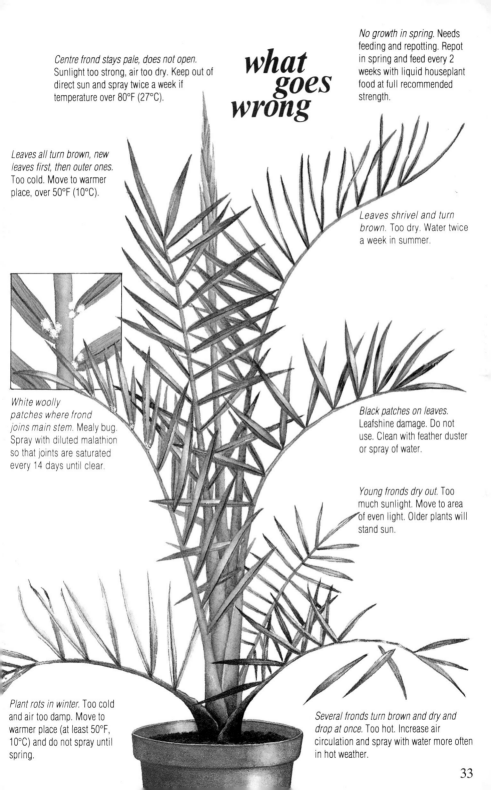

what goes wrong

Centre frond stays pale, does not open. Sunlight too strong, air too dry. Keep out of direct sun and spray twice a week if temperature over 80°F (27°C).

No growth in spring. Needs feeding and repotting. Repot in spring and feed every 2 weeks with liquid houseplant food at full recommended strength.

Leaves all turn brown, new leaves first, then outer ones. Too cold. Move to warmer place, over 50°F (10°C).

Leaves shrivel and turn brown. Too dry. Water twice a week in summer.

White woolly patches where frond joins main stem. Mealy bug. Spray with diluted malathion so that joints are saturated every 14 days until clear.

Black patches on leaves. Leafshine damage. Do not use. Clean with feather duster or spray of water.

Young fronds dry out. Too much sunlight. Move to area of even light. Older plants will stand sun.

Plant rots in winter. Too cold and air too damp. Move to warmer place (at least 50°F, 10°C) and do not spray until spring.

Several fronds turn brown and dry and drop at once. Too hot. Increase air circulation and spray with water more often in hot weather.

33

Date palm

This is the true date palm, growing to 150ft (45m) in its natural habitat. As an indoor plant it will grow to a maximum of 30ft (9m). Its large trunk makes it very heavy, a 12-ft (3½m) specimen weighing about one ton, so that it needs a large room with a strong floor. The long graceful fronds of its leaves are quite rigid and have a razor-sharp spike on the end.

Like the Canary island date palm, it is a slow grower and will take about 6 years to outgrow a normal room. If kept in central heating in winter, it will produce new fronds all year round. This weakens the plant, making it more susceptible to insect pests.

Light: Full sun or high level of indirect light. Artificial lighting will considerably help growth (see p. 13).

Temperature: Winter minimum 50°F (10°C), summer maximum 75°F (24°C) with good ventilation.

Water: At least twice a week in summer to keep evenly moist. In winter water only when surface soil appears dry, about once in 14 days.

Humidity: Hose down with fine mist twice a week if temperature near summer maximum. Edge of indoor swimming pool an ideal situation.

Feeding: Weekly in summer with liquid houseplant food diluted with water according to maker's instructions. (See p. 8.)

Soil: Pure loam/clay mixture. No peat or humus.

Repotting: Only if pot-bound, that is when pot begins to bulge. Plant established specimens into indoor bed at least 4ft (1m) square and 4ft (1m) deep with drainage at bottom. Change topsoil every three or four years.

Cleaning: Spray with tepid soft water. Dust with feather duster. No leafshine.

The Date palm has spear-shaped leaves with a sharp spike on the end. They are quite stiff and can cut badly if they are not handled carefully. Grown quite easily from a fresh date stone, they may grow to an inconveniently large size in about six years.

Removing dead fronds
1. Old fronds gradually dry out and die. Wait until they are quite dried before removing.
2. Cut off as close to trunk as possible, using fine-toothed saw.

Lower fronds dry out and die. Natural for old leaves. Cut off as close to trunk as possible, using a fine-toothed saw.

what goes wrong

Plant does not grow. Needs feeding. Feed weekly in summer with houseplant food at full recommended strength.

New frond turns black. Too cold. Do not allow temperature to drop below 50°F (10°C).

New fronds stay pale and do not develop. Too dark. If you have no lighter place, provide artificial lighting.

Plant dries out, starting with new fronds. Too hot. Do not exceed 75°F (24°C) unless ventilation good.

Tips of leaves dry out. Air too dry. Spray twice a week with fine mist of soft water if hot and dry.

White woolly patches under leaves. Mealy bug. Spray every 14 days with diluted malathion until clear.

Several leaves drop in quick succession. Needs water. Water at least twice a week in summer.

Leaves blotchy. Leafshine damage. Do not use. Clean only with soft water.

Base of trunk rots. Too wet, standing in water. Allow to dry out before watering again.

Pygmy date palm

This is a thin-leaved plant growing from a bulbous stem. New sucker shoots tend to sprout from the base and should be removed or the plant will weaken. Do not confuse these suckers with other plants growing in the same pot, as these palms are often sold two or three to a pot, to give a denser display of foliage. Unlike other *Phoenix* varieties, *P. roebelinii* (sometimes incorrectly called *P. humitis*) does not have sharp leaves on its fronds. New fronds appear from the centre of the plant, growing slightly taller than existing ones. The plant grows only to about 2ft (60cm) high and is relatively easy to care for. Its main requirement is humidity but it dislikes extremes of temperature.

Tho Pygmy dale palm has soft, graceful fronds which appear more delicate and fragile than they actually are. They grow from a bulbous stem and the plants do not normally become large enough to develop a trunk.

Light: Diffused daylight when young (see p. 13). Will grow slowly in shaded position.
Temperature: Winter minimum 55°F (12°C), summer maximum about 70°F (21°C), provided in humid position.
Water: Twice a week in summer, about once every 10–14 days in winter. Plant should almost dry out between waterings in winter.
Humidity: Spray daily with tepid soft water to help humidity. Stand in saucer of pebbles almost covered with water, or put pot into a larger container with damp peat between the two.
Feeding: Every 14 days in summer with liquid houseplant food diluted with water according to maker's instructions.
Soil: 3 parts loam-based No. 2 with 1 part peat.
Repotting: Annually in early spring into clay pot one size larger.
Cleaning: The daily spray for humidity will keep leaves clean. If dusty, wipe carefully with damp cloth. No leafshine.

Fronds dry out and turn crisp. Needs water. Plunge into bucket of water for half an hour, then drain.

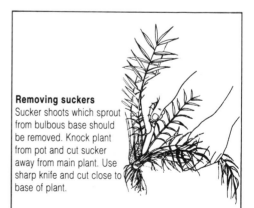

Removing suckers
Sucker shoots which sprout from bulbous base should be removed. Knock plant from pot and cut sucker away from main plant. Use sharp knife and cut close to base of plant.

No new fronds in spring and summer. If early spring, repot. If summer, feed regularly until following spring, then repot.

Young leaves turn brown and dry out before developed. Sunlight too strong. Move to area of diffused daylight until leaves fully develop.

what goes wrong

Small yellowish dots on leaves, webs underneath. Red spider mite. Spray with diluted malathion every 14 days, especially under leaves.

Lower leaves turn brown and dry out. Air too dry. Spray regularly, especially in summer and place pot on wet pebbles.

White woolly patches on leaf joints. Mealy bug. Spray with malathion every 14 days until clear, and add malathion to water for pot every 14 days until clear.

Plant droops, looks lifeless, starts to turn yellow. Too wet, roots stagnating. Allow to dry out before watering again. Water less often in winter than summer.

Fronds turn black and dry out. Leafshine damage. Do not use. Clean with spray of soft tepid water.

Rhapis excelsa

Lady palm

This genus of five species of palm originated in southern China and Japan. Neat and attractive, they form large clusters of delicate slender stems in clumps and grow to a height of about 3ft (90cm). The leaves, growing from the multiple thick cane-like trunks, are divided into between 5 and 7 segments. The bases of old leaves remain to form a covering for the trunk in the form of woven fibres. The trunk is about as thick as a thumb and rod-like. The palm, which is sometimes called the ground rattan cane, should be kept out of strong sun, as this will turn the leaves yellow A variegated variety with yellow and green markings is also sometimes available.

Light: Keep out of sunlight in summer. Full light in winter.
Temperature: Winter minimum 45°F (7°C). Spring and summer temperature of 50–60°F (10–16°C).
Water: Daily in summer, keeping soil constantly moist. Three times a week in winter. Do not stand in water or the roots will become waterlogged.
Humidity: Spray twice daily in summer with tepid soft water to maintain high humidity. Three times a week sufficient in winter. Stand pot on saucer of pebbles almost covered in water, or plant into self-watering container.
Feeding: Weekly in summer with houseplant food diluted with water according to maker's instructions. (See p. 8.)
Soil: Mixture of good loam such as loam-based No. 2 with equal parts of peat and sand. Perfect drainage important.
Repotting: Annually, with plenty of broken crocks in bottom of pot for good drainage.
Cleaning: Humidity spraying adequate. No leafshine.

The Lady palm has smaller leaves than many palms, growing in clusters on delicate, slender stems. They are very sensitive to atmospheric pollution and react badly to any kind of aerosol spray. Healthy plants have glossy green leaves, with no brown or blackened tips.

what goes wrong

Leaves have brown patches. Leafshine or atmospheric pollution. Do not use aerosols of any kind. Keep in fume-free room.

Removing dead fronds
When old leaves dry up and die, cut them off with sharp scissors or secateurs close to main stem.

If leaf tips turn brown and unsightly, clip off ends with scissors. Do not cut into healthy green area.

Webs under leaves, leaves then turn yellow. Red spider mite. Spray every week under leaves with pyrethrum-based insecticide until clear. Water soil once with malathion diluted to half recommended strength.

White woolly patches in leaf joints. Mealy bug. Paint with methylated spirits and remove wool with tweezers. Or water soil with malathion diluted to half recommended strength every 14 days until clear.

Leaf tips fail to open. Needs water and humidity. In summer spray twice a day and water daily.

New leaf tips turn brown. Needs water and humidity. In summer spray twice a day with soft tepid water and water daily.

Brown discs under leaves, marks on surface. Scale insect. Paint under leaves and on stem with methylated spirits and remove with thumbnail.

Leaves turn black. Too cold. Minimum winter temperature 45°F (7°C), or in summer 50°F (10°C).

Irregular chalky white circles on leaves. Lime màrks from spraying with hard water. Use only soft water.

Leaves turn yellow. Too much light. Needs good light but not direct sun.

Older leaves dry out. Natural for old leaves to die one at a time, as new ones produced. If several dry out at same time, too hot or air too dry. Spray twice daily and move to cooler place.

No new leaves appear in growing season. Needs feeding. Feed every week in summer.

Adiantum capillus veneris

Maidenhair fern

This is the most popular variety of maidenhair fern. It requires a humid atmosphere, so generally does well in a steamy kitchen or bathroom with good light. Maidenhair ferns acclimatize themselves to some extent to a particular position, so should not be moved from room to room. If the fronds dry up, the plant can usually be revived if it is cut back just above soil level. If kept moist and humid, new shoots will soon appear. It dislikes cigarette smoke and gas fumes in the atmosphere.

Light: Diffused daylight (see p. 13), not direct sunlight. If only artificial light available fit a horticultural spot light or fluorescent tube (see p. 13).
Temperature: Winter minimum 50°F (10°C), summer maximum 70°F (21°C).
Water: Twice a week in hot weather (over 65°F, 18°C), once a week when cooler, to keep moist at all times. Water by submerging pot until bubbles stop rising, then drain. If plant is in centrally heated room water twice weekly all year round.
Humidity: Spray daily with tepid soft water. Stand on saucer of pebbles almost covered with water or plant pot in larger container with damp peat. Keep away from radiators.
Feeding: Every 14 days in summer only, with houseplant food diluted with water. Use half the amount recommended by the maker. (See p. 8.)
Soil: Use a proprietary soil-less compost containing ready-mixed fertilizer.
Repotting: Every two years only, in plastic pot, as plant likes being pot-bound. Pack new soil loosely round root ball, leaving air gaps. Good drainage essential, so put broken clay pieces or pebbles in pot.
Cleaning: Mist with tepid soft water. No leafshine.

The Maidenhair fern's small green leaves look like miniature versions of the leaves of the Maidenhair tree. A healthy plant should have leaves of a strong green colour, growing closely on the stems. They should show no signs of brown or curling edges.

Leaves dried, brown at edges. Needs watering. Water twice a week all year round if centrally heated. Improve humidity.

Reviving a dried-up plant
1. With scissors, cut out all dried fronds including stems, just above compost.

2. Water by plunging in bucket of water; repeat twice weekly, and spray daily with tepid soft water. Do not feed until new leaves appear.

40

Leaves curl while green. Too wet, may be standing in water. Allow to dry out before watering again and move to a warmer place. Do not feed until plant recovers.

Young leaves turn brown and crisp at tips. Too hot. Do not exceed 70°F (21°C) in summer. Move plant to cooler place where air circulates freely. Spray regularly.

All fronds drop. Kept much too dry for too long; air also too dry. Or gas fumes. Cut down, then water and spray regularly. Keep in fume-free room.

Whole fronds dry out. Air too dry. If not dealt with promptly, all fronds will dry. Spray daily and move away from radiators, boilers etc.

Some leaves turn black. Leafshine damage. Do not use leafshine of any kind. Clean only by spraying with soft water.

Leaves pale. Light too strong. Move to area of diffused light.

what goes wrong

Small flies hopping around soil surface. White fly, attracted by high humidity. Spray every 14 days with pyrethrum until clear. Do not use malathion, leaves will turn black.

Leaves thin, stems weedy. Needs feeding. Feed every 2 weeks throughout summer, using liquid houseplant food at half recommended strength.

Delta maidenhair fern

Not as graceful as *A. capillus veneris*, *A. cuneatum* is more compact, its leaves contrasting in colour with the dark stem. The leaves are coarser than *capillus veneris*, growing more closely together, and the fronds are more upright, making the plant suitable for growing with others in a bowl or planter. This is a much easier plant to care for than other maidenhair varieties since it does not need such constant humidity. It reacts badly to gas fumes or smoke, however, so should be kept away from rooms where these are a problem.

This Maidenhair fern is more compact than *Adiantum capillus veneris* and easier to care for. Its fronds are more upright and the slightly coarser leaves grow more closely together on the stems. Healthy plants should show no signs of dried or discoloured leaves.

Light: High level of diffused daylight (see p. 13). Will survive some distance from a window in semi-shade.

Temperature: Winter minimum 50°F (10°C), summer maximum 75°F (24°C). A cooler position will discourage growth.

Small brown discs under leaves. Not scale insect, but plant's spores or seeds. Can be germinated in heated propagator.

Water: Twice weekly in summer, once a week in winter, to keep evenly moist. Do not allow to dry out.

Humidity: Spray twice weekly with fine mist of tepid soft water. Since *A. cuneatum* is robust, a humid situation not absolutely necessary.

Feeding: Weekly in summer with houseplant food diluted with water according to maker's instructions. (See p. 8.)

Soil: 3 parts peat-based compost with 1 part loam-based No. 2 added.

Repotting: Annually, unless in a bowl with other plants, when topsoil should be changed annually. Put broken crocks, pebbles in pot to ensure good drainage.

Cleaning: Spray with tepid soft water. Use feather duster to remove surface dust, taking care not to damage fairly brittle stems. No leafshine.

Watering
1. Test compost with fingers. If light and crumbly, add water at top of pot, rainwater if possible. Empty excess from saucer after 15 minutes.
2. Or plunge pot into bucket of water and leave until bubbles stop rising. Drain.

42

Leaves curl and drop off. Have you used leafshine? It clogs pores so that leaves cannot breathe. Do not use.

Plant fails to grow or has only small new fronds in summer. Needs feeding or repotting. Check correct compost used.

Leaves drop without warning. Too hot and dry. Move to cooler place and spray regularly.

what goes wrong

Whole fronds die. Insufficient watering, aggravated by gas fumes or smoke in atmosphere. Water more often and move to fume-free room.

Leaves curl but do not drop. Too wet and cold. Move to warmer place and allow compost to dry out before watering again.

Leaves pale. Too much direct sunlight. Move out of sun.

New leaves dry up. Needs water. Water twice a week in summer, when compost should always feel moist.

Small flies hopping on soil surface. White fly. Spray every 14 days with pyrethrum until clear. Do not use malathion or other systemic insecticide or leaves will blacken.

Asparagus falcatus

Thorn fern

This quick-growing fern is easy to care for provided it is watered sufficiently. Upright in habit and growing to a maximum height of about 4ft (just over 1m), it needs careful handling as the thorns on the main stem can scratch. Needing more warmth in winter than other *Asparagus* varieties, it is more suited to central heating, provided reasonable humidity is maintained. It likes porous soil and since this does not hold moisture, it needs to be watered frequently as it must never dry out completely.

Light: Needs plenty, or leaves will remain pale. Full sunlight causes plant to shrivel and die.
Temperature: Best temperature is 55–60°F (12–15°C). Will tolerate 45°F (8°C) but growth slows. Higher temperature in summer will suit, provided ventilation is good. Can be put outside during the day in summer.
Water: As often as necessary to keep moist, especially in summer. Probably 3 times a week in summer, once a week in winter.
Humidity: Spray once a week, daily if over 75–80°F (24–27°C). Planting with other plants in large self-watering container helps local humidity.
Feeding: Weekly when growing with houseplant food diluted with water according to maker's instructions. (See p. 8.)
Soil: Peat-based compost with added fibre (¼ by volume) such as well-rotted leaf mould.
Repotting: In spring, when root system fills pot, and then into plastic pot one size larger. Take care not to damage roots.
Cleaning: Spray with tepid rain or soft water. No leafshine.

The Thorn fern has sharp thorns on its stems. Healthy plants should have leaflets all down the stems and be a good bright green colour with no yellow leaves or brown, shrivelled fronds. They are good plants for centrally heated houses as they do not require very high humidity.

Leaves remain pale. Too dark. Move to lighter place but not full sunlight.

All leaflets drop, leaving bare stem. Plant dried out, needs water urgently. Plunge into bucket of water and leave until bubbles stop rising. Drain before replacing in position.

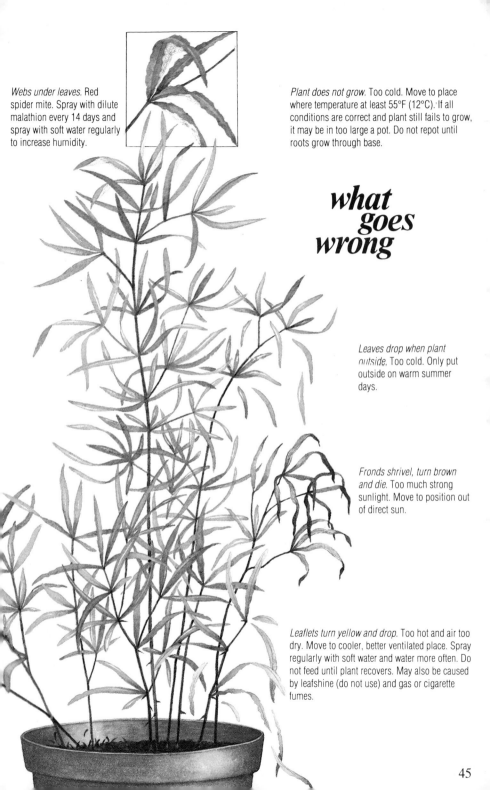

Webs under leaves. Red spider mite. Spray with dilute malathion every 14 days and spray with soft water regularly to increase humidity.

Plant does not grow. Too cold. Move to place where temperature at least 55°F (12°C). If all conditions are correct and plant still fails to grow, it may be in too large a pot. Do not repot until roots grow through base.

what goes wrong

Leaves drop when plant outside. Too cold. Only put outside on warm summer days.

Fronds shrivel, turn brown and die. Too much strong sunlight. Move to position out of direct sun.

Leaflets turn yellow and drop. Too hot and air too dry. Move to cooler, better ventilated place. Spray regularly with soft water and water more often. Do not feed until plant recovers. May also be caused by leafshine (do not use) and gas or cigarette fumes.

Asparagus meyerii

Plume asparagus

This is a wonderfully eye-catching plant which when mature can be 3ft (90cm) in diameter and 2ft 6in (75cm) high. Its long fronds have delicate soft leaflets growing in a bristle-like formation. The root system produces tubers which rest on the top of the pot, and a mature specimen can weigh as much as 56lb (25kg) in a 12in (30cm) pot. A young plant in the shop may be only 12in (30cm) tall and the same in diameter but remember when buying that in 2 or 3 years time it will need almost 3 times as much space.

The Plume asparagus has imposing, upright fronds which look like large bottlebrushes. They can grow to 30in (75cm) long. A healthy plant will have its main stems well covered with side branches, in turn bearing hundreds of tiny leaflets. These may dry and drop if conditions are not right.

Light: Shade suitable, but diffused light needed to help pale green new fronds mature to darker colour (see p. 13). Keep out of direct sunlight.

Temperature: Winter minimum 50°F (10°C), summer best at 55–60°F (12–15°C). If too hot, leaves will drop. Allow good air circulation.

Water: 2 or 3 times a week in summer, to keep moist. Weekly in winter.

Humidity: Mist daily with tepid water. Stand young plant on saucer of pebbles almost covered with water or pot mature plant in self-watering container.

Feeding: Every 14 days in summer only, with houseplant food diluted with water. Use half the amount recommended by the maker. (See p. 8.) In week between feeds, add foliar food to water for one of the daily sprays.

Soil: Loam or peat-based with low-level fertilizer content. Blend loam-based No. 1 half and half with peat.

Repotting: When roots appear through bottom of pot, repot into pot one size larger. Plant a large specimen into self-watering planter.

Cleaning: Spraying and foliage feeding will keep it clean. No leafshine.

what goes wrong

Fronds turn pale, droop and drop leaves. Overwatering. Allow to dry out before watering again.

Humidity
To provide permanent humidity around plant, put damp pebbles or gravel in saucer and stand pot on top. Keep pebbles wet but don't let base of pot actually stand in water.

or
Stand pot in outer container packed with damp peat.

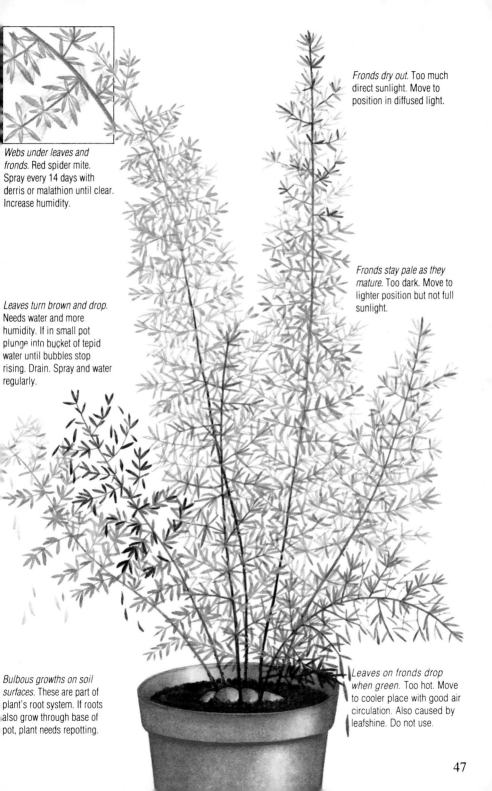

Fronds dry out. Too much direct sunlight. Move to position in diffused light.

Webs under leaves and fronds. Red spider mite. Spray every 14 days with derris or malathion until clear. Increase humidity.

Fronds stay pale as they mature. Too dark. Move to lighter position but not full sunlight.

Leaves turn brown and drop. Needs water and more humidity. If in small pot plunge into bucket of tepid water until bubbles stop rising. Drain. Spray and water regularly.

Bulbous growths on soil surfaces. These are part of plant's root system. If roots also grow through base of pot, plant needs repotting.

Leaves on fronds drop when green. Too hot. Move to cooler place with good air circulation. Also caused by leafshine. Do not use.

Asparagus fern

This is the fern generally used by florists with roses and for buttonholes. Like all *Asparagus* ferns, it is a member of the Lily family. Its foliage is similar to that of the asparagus vegetable and it makes a good houseplant provided it is not left in a very warm room away from windows. It requires a medium level of humidity. The thorns can scratch if care is not taken when cutting foliage or handling the plant. It prefers a clay pot but is often rather difficult to repot since its fibrous roots cling closely to the sides.

Light: Diffused daylight (see p. 13). Will grow in shade though foliage will remain pale. Keep out of direct sunlight.

Temperature: Winter minimum 45°F (8°C), spring and summer minimum 55°F (12°C), maximum 70°F (21°C) with good ventilation.

Water: 2 to 3 times weekly in summer, at least once a week in winter. Must not dry out.

Humidity: Spray daily with fine mist of tepid water when temperature at maximum. Otherwise, at least twice weekly. Stand on saucer of pebbles almost covered with water to help humidity.

Feeding: Every 14 days all summer, with houseplant food diluted with water. Use half the amount recommended by the maker. (See p. 8.)

Soil: Equal proportions of loam-based No. 1 and sterilized peat. Peat-based seed and cutting compost also suitable.

Repotting: When root-ball is compact and roots show through bottom of pot. Use clay pot one size larger and gently remove old soil mixture from roots before potting up. If roots have grown into clay, twist pot around gently until they separate.

Cleaning: Spraying will keep it clean. No leafshine.

The delicate pale green leaflets of the Asparagus fern are often used in flower arrangements. With plenty of daylight, they should have lush, green foliage but direct sun can dry them out. A healthy plant should have a mass of fronds, well covered in feathery leaflets.

what goes wrong

Leaflets drop continuously. Too dark or too hot. Move to cooler, lighter place and spray daily with mist of tepid water.

Fronds remain pale. Too dark. Move to lighter place.

Fronds turn yellow in winter. Overwatered. Allow almost to dry out between waterings. Check not standing in water.

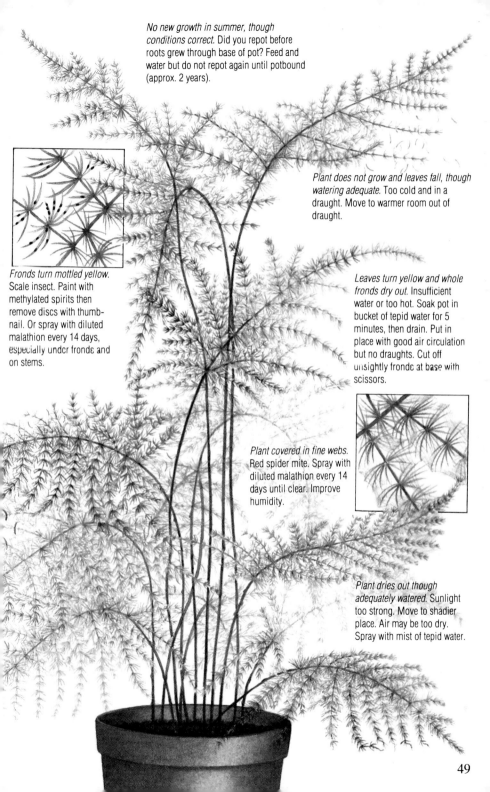

No new growth in summer, though conditions correct. Did you repot before roots grew through base of pot? Feed and water but do not repot again until potbound (approx. 2 years).

Plant does not grow and leaves fall, though watering adequate. Too cold and in a draught. Move to warmer room out of draught.

Fronds turn mottled yellow. Scale insect. Paint with methylated spirits then remove discs with thumbnail. Or spray with diluted malathion every 14 days, especially under fronds and on stems.

Leaves turn yellow and whole fronds dry out. Insufficient water or too hot. Soak pot in bucket of tepid water for 5 minutes, then drain. Put in place with good air circulation but no draughts. Cut off unsightly fronds at base with scissors.

Plant covered in fine webs. Red spider mite. Spray with diluted malathion every 14 days until clear. Improve humidity.

Plant dries out though adequately watered. Sunlight too strong. Move to shadier place. Air may be too dry. Spray with mist of tepid water.

Asparagus

This plant is called by the same common name as *Asparagus plumosus*, but looks quite different. It becomes a bushy plant with fronds both rising and trailing and is the easiest of the *Asparagus* varieties to keep. The foliage lasts well when cut and can be used as table decoration. The leaves are prickly and have sharp needles at the base. *A. sprengeri* is a good plant for the conservatory, kitchen or bathroom. When foliage becomes very overcrowded in the pot, the plant can be divided in spring. The roots are tuberous and you will need a sharp knife to separate them.

Light: Light situation without direct sunlight. Will survive in shade.
Temperature: Winter minimum 45°F (8°C), summer minimum 50°F (10°C). Will take 70–75°F (21–24°C) in summer provided air circulation is good.
Water: 2 or 3 times a week in summer to keep very moist. Water less in winter and allow almost to dry out before watering again, probably once a week.
Humidity: Spray twice a week in summer and once a week in winter with tepid water. Spray even if out-of-doors; if very hot spray daily. Stand on a saucer of pebbles almost covered with water to keep up humidity.
Feeding: Weekly in summer with houseplant food diluted with water according to maker's instructions. (See p. 8.)
Soil: Peat-based compost blended with fertilizer ideal. If using loam-based mixture, choose one with low level of fertilizer (e.g. No. 1) and blend 50:50 with peat.
Repotting: In spring, only if plant seems pot-bound, into clay pot one size larger. Ensure good drainage in pot.
Cleaning: Spraying with water adequate. No leafshine.

This variety of Asparagus fern has spiky, pale green foliage and must not be confused with *Asparagus plumosus*. The fronds are much less filmy, and are in fact quite prickly. They, too, are often used for flower arrangements and last well if cut.

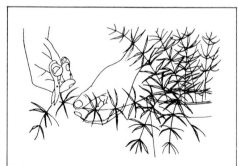

Cutting off dead fronds If dead or damaged fronds are unsightly, cut them off with sharp secateurs or florists' scissors. Cut stem cleanly just above pair of leaves.

Keep fronds healthy by spraying regularly with tepid water. If very hot and dry, stand pot on saucer of damp pebbles to increase humidity.

Plant stops growing. If early summer, did you repot before roots grew through pot base? Do not repot again until pot-bound. If mid to late summer, did you feed through autumn and winter? Plant exhausted. Water but do not feed until following summer.

what goes wrong

Leaflets dry out and drop. Too hot and air too dry. Move to cooler place and increase humidity by spraying or standing pot on wet pebbles.

Leaflets drop though all conditions correct. Leafshine damage or pollution from gas fumes or cigarettes. Move to fume-free room and do not use leafshine.

Leaflets mottled with small discs on undersides. Scale insect. Spray with diluted malathion every 14 days or paint discs with methylated spirits and remove with thumbnail when treated.

Leaflets drop when outside. Too cold or, if in window-box, waterlogged. Bring inside and cut off damaged parts with sharp secateurs or scissors.

Leaflets turn yellow and spines drop. Insufficient water while temperature high or lack of humidity. If over 75°F (24°C) keep plant well watered by plunging pot into bucket of tepid water. Always drain well before replacing pot on saucer.

51

Mother fern

As this attractive plant requires a very humid, though not necessarily hot, atmosphere, it grows best in an enclosed planter, greenhouse or conservatory. Young plants grow on the edge of adult leaves and can be gently removed when well developed and grown into an adult plant. This plant should be bought from a reputable seller as plants kept in normal humidity can soon blacken.

Light: Semi-shade best, though if too dark, plant will not grow. Keep out of strong sunlight.
Temperature: Tolerates winter temperature of 34°F (1°C), though will not grow. Best year-round temperature is 50–65°F (10–18°C). Above 65°F (18°C) plant dries out quickly.
Water: Keep moist at all times, probably watering 2–3 times a week in summer, once a week in winter. Roots rot if plant stands in water, so ensure good drainage in pot. Water less if temperature below about 50°F (10°C), allowing soil almost to dry out between waterings.
Humidity: Spray daily if not in enclosed planter. If in pot, stand on saucer of pebbles almost covered with water.
Feeding: Weekly in summer with houseplant food diluted with water. Use half the amount recommended by the maker (see p. 8). Use a foliar feed instead every week when plantlets developing, again diluted to half the maker's recommended strength.
Soil: Peat-based compost, or 1 part loam-based No. 1 to 2 parts pure peat when two years. Grow plantlets in equal quantities of seed/cutting compost and sharp sand.
Repotting: In spring only when plant looks healthy, into clay pot one size larger. If compost too compressed, roots will rot.
Cleaning: Spray with soft or distilled water. No leafshine.

The Mother fern develops baby plantlets on its fronds. These can be removed and will grow quickly into adult plants. It can survive in a very low winter temperature (though not below freezing) but needs a high level of humidity and is therefore ideal for the enclosed environment of a bottle garden.

Fronds wither. Too much direct sunlight. Move out of sunlight.

Plant turns black in parts, some leaves turn yellow and wither. Air too dry. Spray every day or use terrarium or self-watering planter.

Fronds turn black and die. Leafshine or insecticide not sufficiently diluted. If many fronds affected, plant will die.

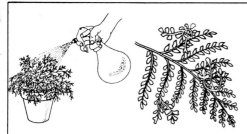

Propagation

1. When plantlets start to appear, give weekly foliar feed at half recommended strength.

2. When plantlets have 2 pairs of leaflets and stem, they are ready for separation.

3. Prepare small pot with layer of drainage and damp compost of ½ sharp sand, ½ peat. Make hole in top with stick or pencil.

4. Pull plantlet gently away from frond with your fingers and place in pot. Press compost lightly around it.

Leaves stay very pale. Needs feeding. Happens particularly when plantlets forming so feed weekly at half recommended strength at this time.

No new growth. Too dark. Move to lighter position.

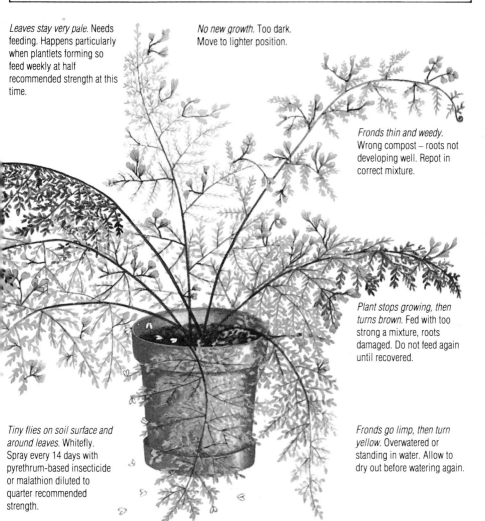

Fronds thin and weedy. Wrong compost – roots not developing well. Repot in correct mixture.

Plant stops growing, then turns brown. Fed with too strong a mixture, roots damaged. Do not feed again until recovered.

Tiny flies on soil surface and around leaves. Whitefly. Spray every 14 days with pyrethrum-based insecticide or malathion diluted to quarter recommended strength.

Fronds go limp, then turn yellow. Overwatered or standing in water. Allow to dry out before watering again.

Asplenium nidus avis

Birdsnest fern

In its natural habitat, this plant grows on trees, obtaining nourishment from rainwater and decaying plant matter around it. Leaves grow from a central point, forming a well. New leaves unfurl delicately into thickish and broad adult leaves. An attractive houseplant, it is relatively easy to grow provided it is not in strong light. In imperfect conditions, older outside leaves become mottled and must be removed at their base with sharp scissors. In a shaded greenhouse or fernery, adult leaves may reach as much as 5ft (1½m) long.

Light: Semi-shaded position to produce healthy leaves. Strong light keeps new growth pale.

Temperature: Winter minimum 55°F (12°C), summer range 70–75°F (21–24°C).

Water: Twice a week in summer, once every 10 days in winter to keep moist at all times. If at minimum temperature in winter, plant should just dry out before being watered again.

Humidity: Plant thrives in moist atmosphere. Spray twice weekly in summer, once weekly in winter. Stand on saucer of pebbles almost covered with water to help maintain humidity.

Feeding: Weekly in summer with houseplant food diluted with water according to maker's instructions. (See p. 8.)

Soil: Peat-based compost. Not loam-based blends.

Repotting: Repot into clay pot in spring only when root-ball seems closely packed. 5in (13cm) pot adequate for 15in (38cm) high plant. It has less root than other ferns.

Cleaning: Spray with soft water, wipe leaves carefully afterwards. No leafshine.

The Birdsnest fern gets its common name from the way the broad leaves radiate from a central well or nest in the middle of the plant. Healthy leaves should be bright, glossy green and there should be new fronds unfurling in the centre.

Humidity

Provide constant humidity by standing pot on saucer of damp pebbles. Do not allow pot base to stand in water.

or

Place in outer pot packed with damp peat.

This plant has a small root system which will probably not grow through base of pot. Examine roots in spring. If they are all growing close together so that soil is obscured, repot in pot one size larger.

what goes wrong

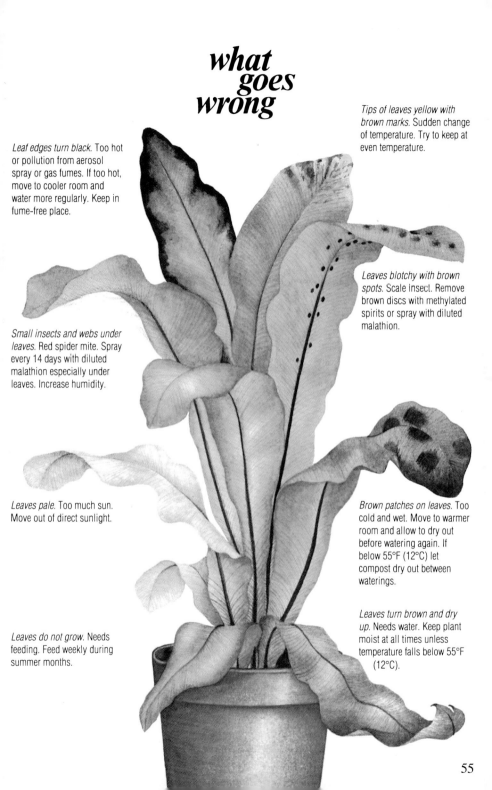

Leaf edges turn black. Too hot or pollution from aerosol spray or gas fumes. If too hot, move to cooler room and water more regularly. Keep in fume-free place.

Tips of leaves yellow with brown marks. Sudden change of temperature. Try to keep at even temperature.

Small insects and webs under leaves. Red spider mite. Spray every 14 days with diluted malathion especially under leaves. Increase humidity.

Leaves blotchy with brown spots. Scale Insect. Remove brown discs with methylated spirits or spray with diluted malathion.

Leaves pale. Too much sun. Move out of direct sunlight.

Brown patches on leaves. Too cold and wet. Move to warmer room and allow to dry out before watering again. If below 55°F (12°C) let compost dry out between waterings.

Leaves turn brown and dry up. Needs water. Keep plant moist at all times unless temperature falls below 55°F (12°C).

Leaves do not grow. Needs feeding. Feed weekly during summer months.

Holly fern

This attractive fern, sometimes also known as the Fishtail fern, is often sold in mixed batches of small ferns. With its glossy, leathery leaves it will thrive in a room where other plants will suffer from smoke or draughts, and is equally happy in the house or an unheated greenhouse. It grows quite rapidly, its fronds reaching 2ft (60cm) long and makes a well-balanced decorative plant. The furry stems grow from an underground rhizome which can be divided in spring. Each section should have roots and 3–4 stems.

Light: Diffused (see p. 13). Does not tolerate direct sunlight.

Temperature: Cool to moderate, 50–65°F (10–18°C) all year round. Remove to coolest part of house if central heating on. Cool greenhouse is ideal.

Water: 3 times a week in summer, once a week in winter; for young plants keep soil always moist.

Humidity: Spray with tepid water twice weekly in summer, once weekly in winter. Provided it is kept cool, requires less humidity than other ferns. Stand on saucer of pebbles almost covered with water if over 65°F (18°C).

Feeding: Weekly in summer with houseplant food diluted with water according to maker's instructions. (See p. 8.)

Soil: Compost of equal parts of loam-based No. 1 or 2, peat and silver sand.

Repotting: Annually up to 7in (18cm) pot, into next size plastic pot, only when rootball fills pot. Do not compress soil too much, or growth will be slowed. If larger, change topsoil in spring.

Cleaning: Spray with solution of 6 or 7 drops of milk in cup of water to clean and give gloss to leaves. Then wipe with soft cloth. No leafshine.

The Holly or Fishtail fern has bright, glossy, leathery leaves which look rather unlike those of a typical fern. These help it to survive in less humid situations than some ferns, and also make it less susceptible to fumes or smoke in the atmosphere. Though shiny, the leaves should never be treated with leafshine.

Leaves turn brown and crisp. Too dry. Water 3 times a week in summer, once a week in winter. Remove dead fronds.

Removing dead fronds
Cut stem of frond at soil level with sharp scissors. Be careful not to damage new shoots.

Cleaning
Mix 6 or 7 drops of milk in a teacup of water and spray or wipe leaves. Remove with a soft cloth.

what goes wrong

Brown burn marks on leaves. Leafshine damage. Do not use. Clean with milk and water mixture (see below).

Leaves turn dull and soft with webs and small insects underneath. Red spider mite. Spray with diluted malathion, especially under leaves. Use weekly for 3 weeks. Increase humidity.

New leaves much smaller than old ones. Needs feeding. Feed every week in summer while growing with houseplant food at full recommended strength.

Leaves pale and no new ones appear. Too dark. Move to lighter place but not full sunlight.

Plant droops. In summer or if central heating high in winter, too hot. Move to cooler place. If temperature correct, check plant is not standing in water. If so, allow to dry out before watering again.

Leaves turn pale and die in summer though conditions seem correct. Too much direct sunlight. Move to shadier place. Continue watering and spraying regularly.

Davallia fijiensis

Rabbit's foot fern

This fern produces a rhizome which hangs over the top of the pot, looking uncannily like a rabbit's foot. Although in it natural habitat, its fronds grow to 18in (45cm), as a houseplant they usually reach only 6–12in (15–30cm). It differs from most ferns in that it should not be sprayed to help humidity and it is sensitive to salt, so should be watered with soft water. The rhizome should not be planted in the soil but raised above soil level and grown over the edge of the pot. They are good plants for hanging baskets as their furry 'feet' make an attractive display.

Light: Good light, near window that does not get full sun best. Keep out of direct sunlight.
Temperature: In summer 64–68°F (18–20°C), reasonably steady 60°F (15°C) in winter.
Water: 2 or 3 times a week in summer, once or twice a week in winter with soft water. Keep soil moist but not soaked.
Humidity: Does not thrive in dry air (e.g. central heating) but do not spray with water. Stand pot on pebbles almost covered with water. A kitchen which is sometimes steamy is ideal.
Feeding: Every 14 days in growing season with liquid houseplant food diluted with water. Use half the amount recommended by the maker. (See p. 8.) No 'plant sticks' or granulated food.
Soil: Compost of 3 parts fibrous peat or well-rooted leaf mould, 1 part chopped sphagnum moss, 1 part silver sand.
Repotting: In spring into clay pot one size larger. Good drainage essential: line pot with broken clay pots.
Cleaning: Dust lightly with feather duster. No leafshine.

A healthy Rabbit's foot fern has slightly glossy leaves but is often bought for its striking, furry-looking rhizomes which hang down over the top of the pot like a rabbit's foot. Unlike most ferns, it should not be sprayed and if it is necessary to treat it with insecticides, these should be added to the soil when watering. Hard water can cause the rhizomes to turn black, so always use soft or rain water.

White mould on stems and leaflets in summer. Mildew. Plant too wet or sprayed, possibly pot-bound. Repot and water once with systemic fungicide.

Leaflets pale, tips turn brown. Too much sun. Keep in light place but not direct sunlight.

Whole fronds turn black. Damage from spraying with either water or insecticide. Do not spray at all.

Leaflets fall in winter. Some leaf loss natural but if all leaflets fall, too cold. Place in warmer room (at least 60°F, 15°C) in winter.

Repotting

1. Carefully remove plant from old pot. Do not damage rhizomes.

2. Mix compost of 3 parts fibrous peat or leaf-mould, 1 part chopped sphagnum moss, 1 part silver sand.

3. Add broken crocks or pebbles to provide drainage in pot 1 size larger.

4. Put layer of compost in new pot and place plant on it. Cover with rest of compost allowing rhizomes to remain above surface.

Whole fronds turn brown. Too hot, air too dry, probably central heating. Keep between 60°F (15°C) and 68°F (20°C). Do not spray but place pot on wet pebbles.

what goes wrong

Plant does not grow. Too dark. Move to area of diffused daylight. If growth stunted and no rhizomes appear, compost too heavy. Repot in spring using suggested compost mixture.

Fronds have black patches and are distorted. Leafshine damage. Clean only with feather duster.

Leaflets turn brown at tips in summer. Humidity too high. Do not spray.

Leaflets shrivel in summer. Direct sunlight. Move to area of diffused light.

Tiny black-winged insects on leaves. Growth stunted. Thrips. Do not spray plant but add systemic insecticide to water every 14 days until clear.

White insects hopping in soil. Whitefly. Add systemic insecticide to water every 14 days until clear. Do not spray plant.

Rhizomes turn black. Hard water used or salt in water. Also caused by plant fertilizer sticks or granulated plant food.

Dicksonia brackenbridgei

Tree fern

Once rare and expensive, this fern is now obtainable through specialist houseplant firms. Even short specimens will grow to a diameter of 6ft (nearly 2m) so it needs space. One of over 20 species of *Dicksonia*, a native of Polynesia, Australia and New Zealand, *D. brackenbridgei* is usually bought 4–5ft (1–1½m) high, and may reach 15ft (4½m) high, though it is a slow grower. It is quite easy to care for provided it is kept moist all year round in a shady place.

Light: Diffused, not direct sunlight (see p. 13).
Temperature: Winter minimum 50°F (10°C), summer maximum 65°F (18°C).
Water: Twice daily in mid-summer, but do not stand in water. Reduce frequency as days shorten; in winter twice weekly should be adequate. Water the trunk, allowing water to run down into pot.
Humidity: Spray with soft water daily in summer (especially the trunk), twice weekly in winter. Conservatory ideal to keep humidity level high.
Feeding: Weekly in summer with houseplant food diluted with water according to maker's instructions. (See p. 8.)
Soil: Best mixture is 2 parts loam-based No. 1, 1 part fibrous peat, 1 part coarse silver sand. Otherwise, equal parts of loam-based No. 1 and peat-based compost.
Repotting: Every two years in spring is sufficient if feeding has been regular. Pot up into plastic pot 2 sizes larger, being careful not to damage trunk or root ball. For large plants, change the topsoil only, in spring.
Cleaning: Spray with soft, tepid water. No leafshine. Keep out of polluted atmosphere.

The Tree fern is a magnificent fern which develops a trunk and long bracken-like fronds. Individual leaflets are quite thick and when healthy, develop a natural dull shine. New fronds grow from a central point, but may also appear as suckers at the plant's base.

what goes wrong

Plant overbalances. Large plants may become top-heavy and because compost is light and fibrous, can easily be knocked over. Repot in pot two sizes larger.

Removing old fronds
When old frond dies, cut it off at base where it joins trunk, with sharp knife.

Watering
In summer, water trunk as well as pot, allowing water to drain down into pot.

New frond dies. Needs water and air too dry. Water twice daily when temperature near summer maximum (65°F, 18°C) and spray daily with soft water.

Leaves blacken and shrivel. Atmosphere polluted, or leafshine. Move to fume-free room and do not use leafshine.

All leaves look dull and lifeless. Plant standing in water. Needs frequent watering in summer but must be well drained.

New frond does not unfurl. Too dark or needs feeding. Keep in light position (not full sun) and feed every week in summer.

Leaves turn pale. Direct sunlight. Keep in light place but not in direct sunlight.

Frond dies. Natural for older fronds to die one by one. Cut back frond at point where it joins trunk.

Insects in trunk. Millipedes. They burrow into trunk, making plant susceptible to disease. Spray trunk with malathion diluted to half recommended strength.

Leaf tips turn black. Too cold or too dark. Keep between 50° and 65°F (10° and 18°C) in good light.

White dots and streaks on leaves. Thrips. Add systemic insecticide to the water every 14 days until clear. Do not spray fronds with insecticide.

Fronds droop. Needs water. In summer water twice daily if temperature 65°F (18°C) or over. Water trunk, allowing water to run into pot.

61

Nephrolepis exaltata

Sword fern

Also known as the ladder fern or Boston fern, this is one of the more common varieties of the large *Nephrolepis* family. It is a good hanging plant and does well planted in a basket. New fronds grow from the centre and uncurl as they develop, and buyers should always look for healthy central foliage. Provided it has sufficient humidity, it is easy to keep, though the ends of the leaves can become ragged if damaged by people brushing past them. In spring it produces plantlets on runners, which root at the edge of the pot. These can be separated to make new plants.

Light: Diffused daylight (see p. 13), though will survive in a quite shady position. Keep out of direct sunlight.
Temperature: Summer minimum 65°F (18°C) and maximum 75°F (24°C). Winter temperatures 55–60°F (13–15°C).
Water: 2 or 3 times a week with soft water in summer to keep moist at all times. Allow almost to dry out in winter before watering, usually once a week.
Humidity: Daily spraying with tepid soft water essential for healthy growth. Stand plant on saucer of pebbles almost covered with water. Bathroom or kitchen good situations for this plant.
Feeding: Every 14 days when growing (spring and summer) with liquid house-plant food diluted with water according to the maker's instructions. (See p. 8.)
Soil: Peat-based compost or 1 part loam-based No. 1 blended with 2 parts sterilized peat.
Repotting: Annually in spring, into plastic pot one size larger. Put broken crocks in pot to provide good drainage.
Cleaning: Spray with soft water. No leaf-shine.

When buying a Sword fern, look for healthy bright green central foliage as new leaves grow from the middle of the plant. Pale green, lush fronds uncurl upwards, developing into a graceful sword shape.

Leaves turn bleached, dry and crisp. Too much direct sun. Move to shadier place.

White deposits on leaves. Lime from spraying with hard water. Use rainwater if possible.

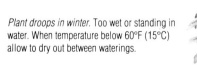

Plant droops in winter. Too wet or standing in water. When temperature below 60°F (15°C) allow to dry out between waterings.

what goes wrong

Leaves turn black. Too cold. Move to warmer room, at least 60°F (15°C) in winter and 65°F (18°C) in summer.

New leaves pale and stunted. Needs feeding. Feed every 14 days in summer when growing. Dilute liquid houseplant food to recommended strength.

Cutting off fronds

1. Cut off brown, shrivelled fronds at base with sharp scissors.

2. If ends of fronds become ragged and dried, cut them off with scissors just inside damaged area. Do not cut into healthy leaf.

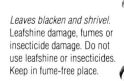

Leaves blacken and shrivel. Leafshine damage, fumes or insecticide damage. Do not use leafshine or insecticides. Keep in fume-free place.

Leaves dry out, shrivel and fall. New fronds in centre brown. Needs water. Cut shrivelled fronds off at base and water well, plunging pot into bucket of water for 1 hour. Drain.

Leaves turn brown at tips, wilt and become crisp. Too hot, air too dry. Move to cooler place and spray daily with tepid soft water.

Pellaea rotundifolia

Button fern

Most ferns in the *Pellaea* family are small and best grown in hanging baskets or indoor rockeries, but *P. rotundifolia* is available in pots. It makes a good houseplant provided it is in a cool to moderate temperature in slight shade with constantly moist soil. Also grows well in a greenhouse or conservatory. Its common name derives from its round, slightly leathery leaves which grow directly from the frond alternately on each side down the length. New leaves grow from the tip of the frond.

Light: Diffused daylight (see p 13). No direct sunlight. Tolerates semi-shade.
Temperature: Tolerates winter minimum of 45°F (7°C). Ideal all-year-round temperature is 55°F (13°C). Summer maximum should be 65°F (18°C).
Water: At least 3 times a week in summer, once or twice a week in winter, as soil must remain moist. Do not water leaves or plant will die. Do not stand in water.
Humidity: Dry atmosphere and airy situation best. High humidity will kill the plant. Do not spray with water.
Feeding: Every 14 days from early spring to mid/late summer with houseplant food diluted with water according to maker's instructions. (See p. 8.)
Soil: Equal parts of loam-based No. 2, leafmould or peat, and crushed limestone. Good drainage is essential as plant must not be waterlogged.
Repotting: Plant has very little root and will grow in 4in (10cm) pot all its life. Change soil every two years and divide if plant becomes top heavy.
Cleaning: Remove dust with feather duster. No spraying, damp cloth or leafshine.

The Button fern's slightly glossy, leathery round leaves grow from a thin brown leaf stem. The leaf edges are slightly crinkled but should not look brown or dried.

Whole fronds dry up. Too dry. Keep soil always moist, watering 3 times a week in summer, twice a week in winter.

Watering and cleaning
Add water from base of pot. Allow to stand for 15 minutes, then empty excess from saucer. Add food to water when feeding.

Clean leaves gently with a feather duster. Do not spray or use leafshine.

Plant does not grow. Needs feeding or, if all conditions are correct, is in too large a pot. Repot in spring into smaller pot. 4in (10cm) is large enough.

what goes wrong

Whole plant turns brown. Too hot. Move to cooler place and keep soil always moist. Cut off brown foliage with scissors as near to soil as possible.

Whole plant goes limp. Bad drainage. Always throw away excess water in saucer after watering.

Individual leaves turn brown and dry up. Atmosphere too humid or leaves wet from spray or watering. Do not spray and water from below.

Leaves turn black and die. Leafshine damage, do not use. Only sprayed leaves will be affected. Cut off leaves close to stem or cut frond close to soil.

Some leaves turn brownish yellow, webs under leaves. Red spider mite. Do not spray but add systemic insecticide to water once a week until pest disappears. Remove webs with feather duster.

Leaves turn black. Too cold. Keep at 55°F (13°C) all the year round.

Fronds dry up from tips, leaves blacken. Direct sunlight. Move to area of diffused light.

Plant looks dull and lifeless, but leaves still green. Too dark. Move to lighter place but not in direct sunlight.

65

Stag's horn fern

This native of Australia is striking in appearance and grows best in a hanging container. It can also be grown on a piece of cork bark. It is natural for the leaves at the base of the main 'horns' to appear brown and crispy: they are sterile leaves developed to support the main leaves. The downlike hair on the main leaves must not be removed or the plant will die. Unlike most ferns, it does not mind a dry atmosphere. It is sometimes difficult to water, as the sterile leaves grow right over the compost with no gaps for the watering can spout to penetrate. The best way of watering is to plunge the pot into a bucket of water once a week or to water from below.

The Stag's horn fern has down-covered green fronds which grow from the centre of the brownish back leaves. The fronds divide rather like the antlers of a stag and make an unusual display, especially if attached to a piece of cork bark or driftwood. Healthy plants should have downy, unmarked green fronds with signs of new ones appearing.

Light: Full light, even sunshine. Hung close to the glass roof, they will shade a greenhouse or conservatory.

Temperature: Winter minimum 60°F (15°C). In summer keep between 65–75°F (18–24°C).

Water: Plunge pot once a week into water, unless pot has a drip tray allowing watering from below. Dry out between waterings.

Humidity: No special treatment as plant stands dry air. If central heating 75°F (24°C) or above, spray once a week with soft water.

Feeding: Once a month in spring and summer with houseplant food diluted with water according to maker's instructions. (See p. 8.)

Soil: 1 part chopped sphagnum moss to 2 parts peat-based compost ideal.

Repotting: Once every two years for young plants. Adult plant has little root and prefers to be left alone.

Cleaning: Spray once a month with soft water, or gently use feather duster. Never wipe leaves. No leafshine.

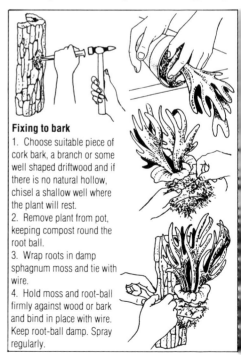

Fixing to bark
1. Choose suitable piece of cork bark, a branch or some well shaped driftwood and if there is no natural hollow, chisel a shallow well where the plant will rest.
2. Remove plant from pot, keeping compost round the root ball.
3. Wrap roots in damp sphagnum moss and tie with wire.
4. Hold moss and root-ball firmly against wood or bark and bind in place with wire. Keep root-ball damp. Spray regularly.

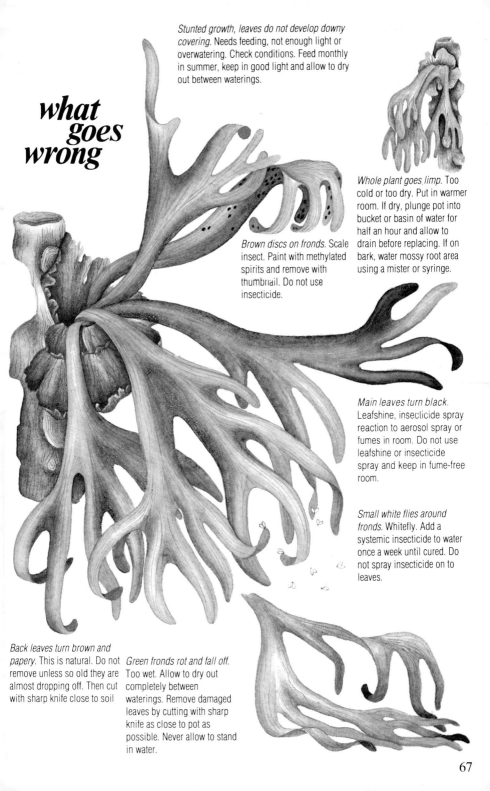

Stunted growth, leaves do not develop downy covering. Needs feeding, not enough light or overwatering. Check conditions. Feed monthly in summer, keep in good light and allow to dry out between waterings.

what goes wrong

Brown discs on fronds. Scale insect. Paint with methylated spirits and remove with thumbnail. Do not use insecticide.

Whole plant goes limp. Too cold or too dry. Put in warmer room. If dry, plunge pot into bucket or basin of water for half an hour and allow to drain before replacing. If on bark, water mossy root area using a mister or syringe.

Main leaves turn black. Leafshine, insecticide spray reaction to aerosol spray or fumes in room. Do not use leafshine or insecticide spray and keep in fume-free room.

Small white flies around fronds. Whitefly. Add a systemic insecticide to water once a week until cured. Do not spray insecticide on to leaves.

Back leaves turn brown and papery. This is natural. Do not remove unless so old they are almost dropping off. Then cut with sharp knife close to soil

Green fronds rot and fall off. Too wet. Allow to dry out completely between waterings. Remove damaged leaves by cutting with sharp knife as close to pot as possible. Never allow to stand in water.

Platycerium grande

Elk's horn fern

The variety 'Queen Wilhelmina', the one most usually available, has fronds which tend to grow over the pot, eventually covering it up completely. The plant is a little difficult to grow but very rewarding, as from the side it looks like a mounted elk's horn trophy hanging on a wall. Since *P. grande* is susceptible to damage in handling, it is best to buy a young plant which will eventually grow into a specimen some 18–24in (45–60cm) in diameter.

Light: Well-lit room with diffused daylight (see p. 13). A conservatory is ideal.
Temperature: Winter absolute minimum 65°F (18°C). In summer, 65–75°F (18–24°C).
Water: Weekly all year round. Best done from below by standing pot in water for half an hour and allowing to drain.
Humidity: Does not mind the dry atmosphere of the home but can be seen at its best in heated conservatory or greenhouse at 60° humidity.
Feeding: Once a month in spring and summer by adding liquid houseplant food to water before standing pot in it. Dilute food according to maker's instructions. (See p. 8.)
Soil: Equal parts of chopped sphagnum moss and peat-based compost.
Repotting: Only young plants (1–2 years old), and in spring before back leaf has covered the pot. Once the back leaves have grown over the pot it is almost impossible to remove the plant without damaging it.
Cleaning: Spray once a month with soft water, or use feather duster very carefully. Do not wipe leaves. No leafshine. It will kill the plant by damaging its downy surface.

The Elk's horn fern has larger, less divided leaves than the Stag's horn fern. The horn is part of the base leaf and new, pot-enveloping leaves grow one by one from the centre, each one almost covering the one before. Healthy fronds should have a fine whitish down which should not be removed.

Leaves shiny in parts. Downy surface removed by cleaning or spraying. Move to light, humid place to recover. Small patches will scar fronds. If many fronds affected, plant will die.

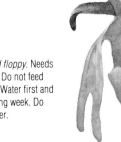

New fronds rot. Overwatered. Allow to dry out in warm place (70°F, 21°C) before watering again.

Fronds thin and floppy. Needs water and food. Do not feed bone dry plant. Water first and feed the following week. Do not feed in winter.

New fronds stay small and pale. Too dark. Needs plenty of light, but not full sun.

what goes wrong

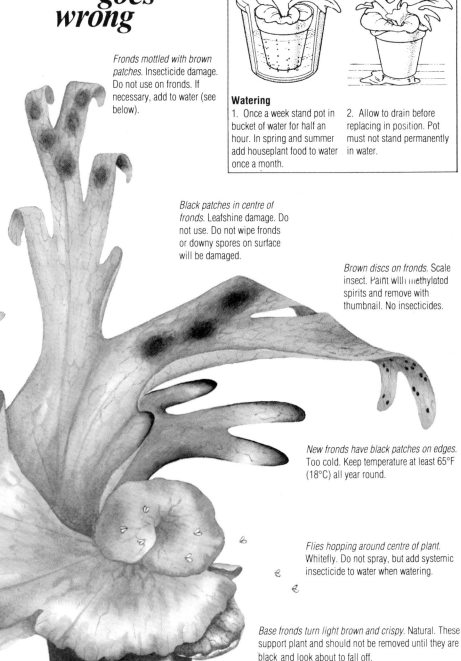

Fronds mottled with brown patches. Insecticide damage. Do not use on fronds. If necessary, add to water (see below).

Watering

1. Once a week stand pot in bucket of water for half an hour. In spring and summer add houseplant food to water once a month.

2. Allow to drain before replacing in position. Pot must not stand permanently in water.

Black patches in centre of fronds. Leafshine damage. Do not use. Do not wipe fronds or downy spores on surface will be damaged.

Brown discs on fronds. Scale insect. Paint with methylated spirits and remove with thumbnail. No insecticides.

New fronds have black patches on edges. Too cold. Keep temperature at least 65°F (18°C) all year round.

Flies hopping around centre of plant. Whitefly. Do not spray, but add systemic insecticide to water when watering.

Base fronds turn light brown and crispy. Natural. These support plant and should not be removed until they are black and look about to fall off.

Polypodium aureum

Hare's foot fern

The hare's foot fern grows from a furry rhizome which lies half buried in the compost and in time spreads over the surface of the pot. New stems emerge tightly coiled and unfurl to grow into long, brownish, slender stalks up to 2ft (56cm) long, bearing elegant green fronds which add another 16–20in (40–50cm) to the total length. On the undersides of the fronds small orange-brown spores appear on either side of the central vein. Fronds die away one by one and are replaced by new growth from the rhizome.

Light: High level of diffused light essential (see p. 13). Keep out of direct sunlight.
Temperature: 55–65°F (13–18°C) from early spring to late autumn. Hotter than 70°F (21°C), the leaves will shrivel. Winter minimum 50°F (10°C)
Water: 3 times a week in summer to keep soil moist and once or twice a week in winter, allowing top ½in (1cm) to dry out between waterings. Do not stand in water or expose plant to continual dripping of water.
Humidity: Spray daily with tepid soft water from late winter to early autumn. Stand pot in saucer of pebbles almost covered with water.
Feeding: Every 14 days in summer only, with liquid houseplant food diluted with water. Use half the amount recommended by the maker. (See p. 8.)
Soil: Equal parts of loam-based No. 2, peat, leafmould and coarse potting sand.
Repotting: In spring into pot two sizes larger, since rhizomes can spread to cover whole surface of compost. Every 2 or 3 years divide rhizomes and repot into well-drained 5in (13cm) pots. Each section of rhizome should have roots and 2–3 stems.
Cleaning: Spray daily with soft water. No leafshine.

The Hare's foot fern has graceful, bright green fronds on long stems which are green when young, but turn brown as they grow. The stems emerge from a furry rhizome which lies half buried in the compost and will spread to cover the pot surface. Healthy leaves should look bright and fresh and in spring and summer may have lines of orange spores on the undersides.

Humidity
1. Provide constant humidity around pot by standing pot on saucer of pebbles, half covered in water. Do not allow base of pot to touch water.
2. Or, place pot in outer container packed with damp peat.

70

No new growth in spring though all conditions correct. Soil too heavy. Repot using correct mixture.

what goes wrong

Stems too crowded in pot, rhizome fills pot. Needs repotting or dividing. Do this every 2–3 years in spring.

New leaves pale. Too dark. Needs good diffused daylight but not direct sun.

Tips of fronds turn black. Food too strong. Feed only every 2 weeks in growing season and use food diluted at half recommended strength.

Foliage dries up and turns brown. Air too dry. Spray daily with water and provide extra humidity by standing on wet pebbles. Or keep in steamy bathroom or kitchen.

Fronds begin to rot away. Too wet or standing in water. If using wet pebbles to provide humidity, make sure pot base is clear of water.

Fronds turn black and shrivel. Leafshine damage. Do not use. Clean only by spraying with soft tepid water.

Plant wilts. Too dry and too hot. Keep soil moist and water daily in summer. Move to cooler place (70°F, 21°C maximum).

Flies hopping around soil surface. Whitefly. Add pyrethrum-based insecticide to water every 14 days until clear. Do not use malathion and do not spray leaves.

Leaflets dry up one by one. Too much direct sunlight. Move to shadier place. Do not spray in sunlight.

Ribbon fern

Over 250 species of *Pteris* exist. *P. cretica* is a robust-looking variety, and is quite easy to keep in the home provided it is kept moist at all times. *P. cretica albolineata* is a variegated version of the species which is delicately marked with a pale centre to the broad leaflets. *Pteris* has fairly thick leaves and will take a good deal of neglect. When buying it, look for healthy, undamaged foliage.

Light: Diffused light best, though will survive in a very shaded position. Keep out of sunlight. *P. cretica albolineata* needs less light than other variegated plants and dislikes direct sun.

Temperature: Winter minimum 50–55°F (10–13°C), summer maximum 70°F (21°C).

Water: Daily in summer, 2 or 3 times a week in winter, to keep soil always moist. Do not stand in water.

Humidity: Spray daily with tepid soft water to keep as humid as possible. Stand on a saucer with pebbles almost covered in water or put pot into outer container with damp peat between the two. The more humid the atmosphere, the more healthy the plant.

Feeding: Every 14 days in summer only, with houseplant food diluted with water. Use half the amount recommended by the maker. (See p. 8.)

Soil: Compost of 1 part loam-based No. 1, 2 parts sterilized peat, 1 part sharp sand. Peat-based compost will also suit.

Repotting: Every spring into one size larger plastic pot. Do not firm new compost down too much or roots will be stifled.

Cleaning: Spray with soft water. Be very careful if wiping leaves as the frond stems are very brittle and break easily. No leafshine. Plant is very susceptible.

This is the variegated version of the normal green Ribbon fern, having a narrow white centre stripe down its leaves. Although the leaves look delicate, they are actually quite thick and tough and will tolerate a wide variety of light and temperature conditions. Healthy plants will have several stems growing together with bright leaves showing no signs of discoloured tips.

what goes wrong

Small brown discs on back of leaves. Scale insects. Paint with methylated spirits and remove with thumbnail. For other insects add pyrethrum-based insecticide to water every 14 days until clear. No malathion.

Leaves turn black. Leafshine damage or polluted atmosphere. Clean only by spraying and do not use aerosols in same room as plant.

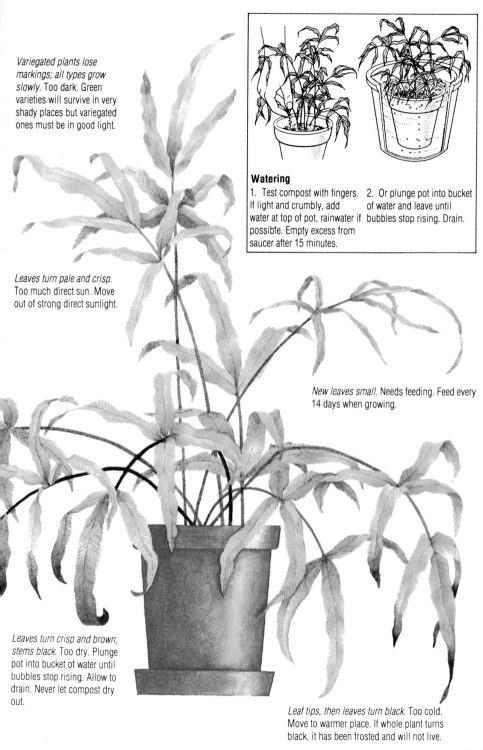

Variegated plants lose markings; all types grow slowly. Too dark. Green varieties will survive in very shady places but variegated ones must be in good light.

Watering
1. Test compost with fingers. If light and crumbly, add water at top of pot, rainwater if possible. Empty excess from saucer after 15 minutes.

2. Or plunge pot into bucket of water and leave until bubbles stop rising. Drain.

Leaves turn pale and crisp. Too much direct sun. Move out of strong direct sunlight.

New leaves small. Needs feeding. Feed every 14 days when growing.

Leaves turn crisp and brown, stems black. Too dry. Plunge pot into bucket of water until bubbles stop rising. Allow to drain. Never let compost dry out.

Leaf tips, then leaves turn black. Too cold. Move to warmer place. If whole plant turns black, it has been frosted and will not live.

73

Pteris cretica crispata

Crisped ribbon fern

The 'cockscomb' leaflet ends and the irregularly-shaped leaves on this extra-ordinary houseplant make for an interesting fern which is quite easy to care for. Like the other species of *Pteris* it derives its name from the Greek word 'pteron', a wing. They need humidity and moisture all the year round but although the soil should never dry out, it must not become heavy and water-logged. Make sure the drainage is good and do not try to save watering by leaving water in the plant's saucer.

Light: Shade preferred, though will stand some strong light. A room that does not get full sun is ideal.
Temperature: Winter minimum 50–55°F (10–13°C), summer maximum 70°F (21°C). Will stand slightly higher if humidity level is high.
Water: Daily throughout summer, about once a week in winter, but plant must never dry out completely. Do not stand in water.
Humidity: Spray daily with tepid soft water all summer and in winter too if plant is in centrally heated room – otherwise, twice weekly adequate. Stand on saucer of pebbles almost covered with water to maintain essential high humidity.
Feeding: Every 14 days in summer with houseplant food diluted with water. Use half the amount recommended by the maker. (See p. 8.) In winter feed once a month if temperature near 70°F (21°C).
Soil: Peat-based compost or mixture of 2 parts loam-based No. 2 and 1 part sand.
Repotting: Annually in spring into plastic pot one size larger. Put plenty of broken crocks for drainage into pot.
Cleaning: Humidity spraying usually adequate, though excess dust may be removed with feather duster. No leafshine.

The pale green, slightly glossy leaves of the Crisped ribbon fern end in leaflets shaped like a cockscomb. On healthy plants, these should be a good bright green, like the rest of the frond, and should not be shrivelled or brown. This is a good plant for a room that never receives full sun as it prefers shade.

what goes wrong

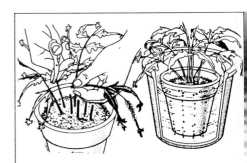

Reviving a dried-up plant
If whole plant dries up from persistent underwatering or dry air, cut off all brown fronds close to soil. Do not damage healthy stems.

Plunge pot into basin of water for 15 minutes, then allow to drain. Repeat daily until plant revives. Do not feed until growing again.

74

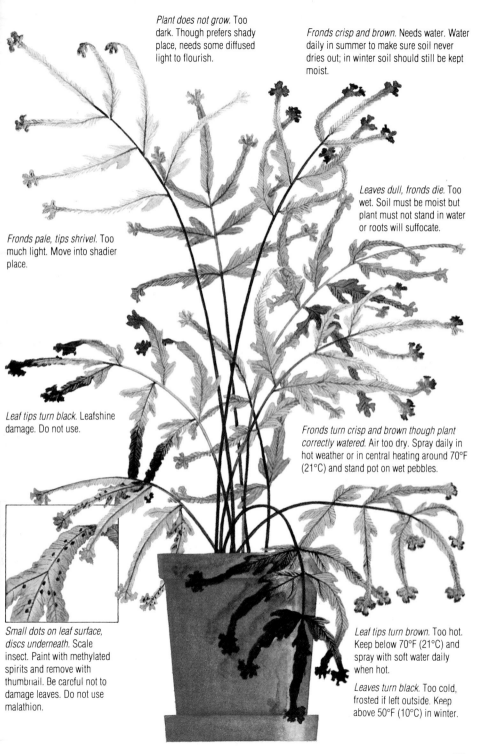

Plant does not grow. Too dark. Though prefers shady place, needs some diffused light to flourish.

Fronds crisp and brown. Needs water. Water daily in summer to make sure soil never dries out; in winter soil should still be kept moist.

Leaves dull, fronds die. Too wet. Soil must be moist but plant must not stand in water or roots will suffocate.

Fronds pale, tips shrivel. Too much light. Move into shadier place.

Leaf tips turn black. Leafshine damage. Do not use.

Fronds turn crisp and brown though plant correctly watered. Air too dry. Spray daily in hot weather or in central heating around 70°F (21°C) and stand pot on wet pebbles.

Small dots on leaf surface, discs underneath. Scale insect. Paint with methylated spirits and remove with thumbnail. Be careful not to damage leaves. Do not use malathion.

Leaf tips turn brown. Too hot. Keep below 70°F (21°C) and spray with soft water daily when hot.

Leaves turn black. Too cold, frosted if left outside. Keep above 50°F (10°C) in winter.

75

Australian bracken

The fronds of this plant are similar to common bracken though less leathery and much smaller. The maximum length of the fronds is about 18in (50cm), whereas bracken grows to 48in (over 1m) and cannot be grown in pots. *P. tremula* makes a most attractive potted fern, with its delicate leaflets bushing out to make a symmetrical plant. The fronds are liable to snap off if accidentally brushed against. If it grows too bushy for its pot, it can be divided in spring by gently pulling the roots and stems apart.

Light: Diffused light out of direct sunlight. (see p. 13.)

Temperature: Winter minimum 50°F (10°C), summer maximum 70°F (21°C), or slightly higher if humidity is high, as in a greenhouse or conservatory.

Water: Daily in summer and 2 or 3 times a week in winter to keep moist at all times. Do not stand in water.

Humidity: Spray daily with tepid soft water, and stand pot in saucer of pebbles almost covered with water. Better still, plant pot into larger pot with damp peat in between or into self-watering planter. High humidity is essential for successful growth. Instructions for using a self-watering planter are on p. 12.

Feeding: Every 14 days in summer and once a month in winter with houseplant food diluted with water. Use half the amount recommended by the maker. (See p. 8.)

Soil: Mixture of 1 part loam-based No. 1, 2 parts sterilized peat, 1 part sharp sand. Can also use peat-based compost.

Repotting: Annually in spring into plastic pot one size larger.

Cleaning: Humidity spraying should be adequate. Soft summer rain, above 55°F (13°C), washes leaves well. No leafshine.

Australian bracken ferns look like miniature versions of wild bracken. Healthy fronds are bright green but shrivel and turn black or brown if conditions are too hot and dry. The spores grow easily and may self-sow beside the parent plant or in the pots of other plants nearby.

Leaflets turn brown and shrivel. Too dry. Keep soil moist always. If many fronds die, cut them off close to soil and plunge pot into basin of water every day for 15 minutes until new growth appears. Allow to drain.

Humidity
Humidity is especially important for this plant. Spray daily in hot weather and provide constant humidity by putting in outer pot packed with damp peat.

Tips of leaflets shrivel then turn black, young leaflets especially affected. Too hot and dry. Spray regularly and move to cooler place.

New leaflets small and do not develop same shape as adult ones. Needs feeding.

Foliage looks burned, with blackened fronds. Leafshine or malathion have damaged leaves. Do not use.

Leaflets pale, growth slow and distorted. Too dark. Move to lighter place but not direct sunlight.

Leaflets turn black from tips. Too cold. Move to warmer place. If whole plant turns black at same time, frosted. Will not recover.

Small white insects fly around plant. Whitefly. Spray every 14 days with pyrethrum-based insecticide until clear.

Small brown discs on leaflets. Scale insect. Paint with methylated spirits and remove with thumbnail. Do not use malathion.

Fronds pale with shrivelled leaflets. Too much direct sun. Move to shadier place with some diffused light.

what goes wrong

Selaginella uncinata

Rainbow moss

Looking like growing moss, *Selaginella* (also known as Peacock fern) can be grown in soil or on cork bark. Without a very humid atmosphere, however, they will turn brown and die. Thus, an ideal situation for them is a bottle garden or fern case where the humidity is constantly high and the plant is protected from draughts. A number of varieties are available, most of them in varying shades of green, though some have a decidedly blue tinge. If the plant grows very quickly it can be cut back by half without damage. Any fronds and leaflets that dry up can also be trimmed off.

Rainbow moss grows as a mass of spreading bright green fronds and when healthy, will have no sign of brown or shrivelled leaflets. The shimmering colour which is caused by light bouncing off its minute scale-like leaves gives it its alternative name of the Peacock fern.

Light: Medium light for successful growth. Do not keep in a dark corner, in a very light position or in full sunlight.

Temperature: Winter minimum 55°F (13°C), summer maximum 65°F (18°C).

Water: Daily in spring and summer unless in fern case or bottle garden. Once a week in winter. Must be kept moist at all times.

Humidity: Very high level essential for successful growth. Steamy kitchen would be suitable, though fern case, cool greenhouse ideal. Keep out of very dry room where even daily spraying would be insufficient.

Feeding: Every 14 days in summer only with houseplant food diluted with water. Use half the amount recommended by the maker. (See p. 8.)

Soil: Peat-based compost mixed with one-third by volume of chopped sphagnum moss to ensure open mixture.

Repotting: Every two years in spring, into well-drained pot. If in fern case or bottle garden, replace some of top soil with fresh compost mixture.

Cleaning: Spray with tepid soft water. Do not use a feather duster as this could break brittle stems. No leafshine.

Tips of fronds shrivel. Too dry. Needs watering every day in growing period.

Some leaflets on frond turn black and die. Leafshine damage. Do not use.

Leaflets and stems black. Too cold. In winter 55°F (13°C) minimum. Place in warmer room and keep humidity high. Remove unsightly stems with scissors.

Fronds turn brown all at once and whole plant dries out. Too hot. Move to cooler place (not more than 65°F, 18°C) if possible.

Leaflets remain pale. Too dark. Move to lighter place but not in direct sun.

Replacing top soil in bottle garden.

1. Carefully remove top inch (2½cm) soil using wooden spoon on end of cane.

2. Add new compost and firm around plant with cotton reel tied to cane.

what goes wrong

Fronds dry up, starting at tip and gradually going black. Direct sun. Move to shadier place.

Small flies around soil surface. Whitefly. Add systemic insecticide to water every 14 days until clear. Do not spray leaves or they will 'burn'.

Plant looks 'tired' and dull. Soil too compact, preventing healthy root development. Repot in correct mixture.

Leaflets brown and shrivelled. Insufficient humidity. Needs very damp atmosphere. Spray daily and place pot on wet pebbles.

Leaflets do not grow. Needs feeding. Feed every 14 days in summer with houseplant food at half recommended strength.

Buying your houseplant

Florists, garden centres and specialist shops are best for unusual plants, large specimens and planted arrangements. Supermarkets, stores and service stations often offer excellent value in popular plants and rely on fast turnover to maintain quality. Market stalls may appear to offer good value but take care, especially in winter, when cold may affect the plants badly.

It is important before buying to consider where the plant is to go. Think about the room conditions, the light, heat or draughts that the plant may be subjected to. If you are a beginner choose a plant that is simple to grow. Don't be tempted to buy one that is exotic until you have had some experience.

Look carefully at the one you intend to buy. It should be firm in its pot, which should be clean. The compost on top should be fresh, not sprouting weeds or moss. None of the leaves should be marked, torn, yellow or faded. Beware of small plants in large pots; this probably means that they have just been repotted and the roots will not have grown properly into the fresh compost.

Always insist, particularly in winter, that the plant you buy is properly wrapped up, if necessary with a double layer of paper. Large plants often require support, with an extra cane to protect the growing tip. Take care not to knock it on the way home. Lastly, make sure you know the plant's correct name so that you can look up its care instructions when you get home. Common names vary from place to place; the scientific name is the most reliable to use for identification.

Acknowledgements

Colour artwork by Jane Fern/The Garden Studio
Line artwork by Patricia Newton (pp. 1–5), Norman Bancroft-Hunt (pp. 6–14), Glen Steward (pp. 15–78)
Photographs by David Cockroft
Plants by courtesy of Thomas Rochford & Son Ltd, Longmans Florists and the Royal Botanic Gardens, Kew
Additional photographs supplied by the A-Z Botanical Photographic Collection
Designed by Marion Neville
Typeset by Faz Graphics